# STUDIOS
## Architecture

# STUDIOS
## Architecture
### The Power of the Pragmatic

*Introduction by*
*James S. Russell, AIA*

l'ARCAEDIZIONI

*Cover Photo:*
3Com Corporation
Dublin, Ireland
© Chris Gascoigne

**Editorial Director USA**
Pierantonio Giacoppo

**Chief Editor of Collection**
Maurizio Vitta

**Publishing Coordinator**
Franca Rottola

**Graphic Design**
Stefano Tosi

**Editing**
Martyn J. Anderson

**Colour-separation**
Litofilms Italia, Bergamo

**Printing**
Poligrafiche Bolis, Bergamo

First published October 1999

Copyright 1999
by l'Arca Edizioni

ISBN 88-7838-056-3

# Contents

# A Roundtable Discussion

*A roundtable discussion was conducted at Studios Architecture, San Francisco, California, May 1998 by Peter Lipson.*
*Mr. Lipson is an architect with Studios and a writer.*

*Q. How did this diverse group come together as a firm called Studios?*

Gene Rae: There was a desire on the part of the original five partners to pursue careers that were more meaningful to them; more meaningful in the delivery of good ideas to clients. The concept of Studios was one in which individuals could set up their own thinking and then hopefully correspond and communicate with others about disparate ideas.

Erik Sueberkrop: Initially it was to have a collaboration, to have thoughts that jumped off of each other, and to have a business net that allowed each partner to work over the humps and bumps—to create a business ideal that protected creative thought.

*Q. Why the name Studios?*

Darryl Roberson: When we came together to start the new firm, there were a lot of questions about whose name would come first—who would have seniority—and we felt that coming together should be open-ended. The question was the individual versus the group, and we decided on the group. We believed the individuals behind Studios would print through the name.

*Q. What holds the partners and the members of the five offices together today?*

David Sabalvaro: That is a question we always try to answer whenever we have a partners meeting: Why are we together? I think it is sharing a passion for design—a desire to seek out design opportunities, but in an organization that allows each individual to explore his own

interests. We are very different personalities, but we share a good degree of respect among the partners.

Charles Dilworth: There was a certain commonality of interests that was based on long personal relationships and which has more recently grown to include other people, and in other offices. It's grown to include someone like myself. There is strength in the group, both in terms of being able to bolster one another up, help each other's practices, and also in terms of business. Clients like firms with more than one lead person.

Pierre Pastellas: Studios doesn't really believe in hierarchy, so the philosophy is what binds us together—because we share the same vision of opportunities, of working with the same type of clients, of doing great design.

Bruce Danzer: At the same time, everyone brings a different perspective to the projects, and this allows for rapid responses that can address the demands and the increasing complexity of our clients' needs. We have a diverse partnership.

Erik: The suggestion here is to try to put together diverse energy and for each of us to get the symbiotic energy from the partnership. That's also true for the constituency beyond the partners. What's happened over the years is that, although there has been some successful collaborations on the design effort of partners, a lot of the design direction has been more a single partner with a studio than was initially envisioned. However, there's a synergistic effect that happens just by having the diversity of people in the office, so that even though we don't all think the same we get nourishment from being around each other. The diversity in the partners and the offices brings out the diversity in the staff. I had an office meeting yesterday with our staff in London, and as a result there's a stimulus in different ways of thinking and different experience bases that we couldn't as easily have if our office was just in San Francisco.

*Q. What are some of the fundamental shared values?*
Phil Olson: We believe in innovation as an underlying cornerstone of everything we think about. This results in challenging how we do things every step of the way. I think our process is by its own nature the essence of innovation, because we're constantly challenging ourselves and how we do things in order to arrive at a greater good.

Charles: We value balance, and it's sometimes a very delicate balance, between a kind of problem-solving and our commitment to raising the level of dialogue. Sometimes it's intrinsic—where every discussion is dedicated to both of these things simultaneously, and sometimes it's a question of oscillating back and forth between the two.

*Q. How important is the collaboration with the client?*
Phil: I would rate the collaboration level very high. As long as there is an underlying sense of purpose and an extraordinary level of professionalism, and a strong design ethos, then collaboration can be, and has been, very effective for us. We're engaging the client in the process of design more effectively than any firm I'm familiar with.

Pierre: The client is definitely part of the team.
Todd: Essentially, the people that hire us are people who want to collaborate. What we've done best in building a practice is choosing clients who will benefit from how we think and our processes.

*Q. Tell me about Studios' process.*
Erik: I think the process is exploratory; it's risk taking, although not for its own sake, but from a standpoint of exploration. What does it look like if you turn it upside down? We don't approach each project with the set method that a number of offices have—our projects are approached in a diverse fashion and mainly get their stimulants from the uniqueness of the client and/or the problem. There's sometimes confusion among junior people in the office because they don't sense a single definitive process. Many of the partners celebrate that because it creates a vigor that allows for exploration. It's looking in the eye of the storm with pleasure and anticipation, rather than dread.

Gene: Bring us complex, programmatic perspectives; bring us qualitative problems, quantitative problems, metaphysical problems; postulate about the future of human ecology; fool around with thinking on the relationship of society and the built environment—all of that can be larded into a thinking process at Studios and have an articulated result, have a result that is made true in form.

Tom: We actively seek out the creative opportunities in a project and explore them to a level where they can

become a pure idea. As a project matures and becomes reality then there are all these functional needs and practical things like having to get it built and getting approved and getting a budget, but at the end of the day I think the thing that really drives all of us is knowing that at the very beginning there was an idea that drove that project.

*Q. Where do the opportunities come from?*
Gene: Where we really thrive is where a client, with our help or without, can articulate a set of values or principles or problems or a business direction, and then let Studios work on how to form that.

Charles: Clients that allow you to take risks are central because if you have a client who fires you the first time you do something they haven't seen before, that kind of stops the process. There are people who start out as good clients and there are people who become good clients through the process.

Pierre: Some clients are willing to take some design risks and some are not. We are obviously there to take advantage of any design opportunity when it's offered, but we don't take risks and then not share them with the client. Clients who are facility and management oriented have particular needs that don't allow for a lot of risk.

*Q. How has Studios achieved the risk taking?*
Todd: The work doesn't usually try to please everybody; I think that's what really comes about from typical corporate design. Nobody ever really hated beige, nobody ever really loved it, but more importantly nobody hates it.

Gene: To a certain extent the risks are really being taken by the client. And to the extent that we understand those risks and can share in the solution, then we are contributing.

Bruce: It seems that design excellence and a successful collaboration with clients are linked. Without one signature design vocabulary, Studios has had to focus on how design contributes to specific client objectives.

Tom: We've all been in experiences elsewhere where we've tried to do leading edge design and the client is not impressed—either does not understand it as well or is not completely committed to it—and the projects end up being compromised, or you can create a schism in the relationship.

Darryl: I think the clients come to us because they are looking for us to push the design. The clients usually hire us for the right reasons.

*Q. Are the clients, then, at the heart of the design process?*
Erik: If we are speaking to corporate work, it ends up being a question of their culture, their philosophy, their way of working; how they want to position themselves for their staff; how they want their staff to live; how they want to celebrate the act of what they're doing—be it creating software, or a sense of family within the company; how they want to be depicted to their clients and to the business community. All these are energy sources for the architecture—they can be ignored or they can be harnessed. These are qualitative agendas that architecture can speak to in a higher vein. Corporate America's experience for a long time here has

been to build a box derived by economy. Is that good enough? Do you want to just make do, versus here's an environment that can cost you the same, but that is being directed to working better and being a better experience for how one goes about their daily affairs.

*Q. What makes the work transcend typical corporate design?*
Charles: I'd say that we've been in search of new typologies, and that is a very architectural act. If you talk about office work being commercial art, some people rail against that and push the envelope. Critics may say that we ripped through the envelope successfully and achieved high art and others think that we're still trapped inside, but we do this because we enjoy it and it interests us.

Gene: Architecture as a high art is an odd dialogue. I don't claim that anything we've done, or that anything most architects have done falls into the area of high art.

Charles: This is a big discussion that happens around here a lot; what's low art, what's high art and it's an ongoing discussion.

*Q. What is the relationship between the work and the corporate clients?*
David: The corporate clients that seek our work are looking for people that can help them speak about their business. It's always in business and corporate terms—using design to their benefit—they're looking to leverage our design to their benefit and we're looking to have the opportunity to use design that works for us. Yet I think the beauty is we've been able to meld with corporations that have a common appreciation for

design. There are some very strong agendas, but I think we can use that to our advantage as well. I think that's why our work is satisfying.

Pierre: On the other hand, some clients start with real estate as a commodity, and it's got to be disposable. Therefore it's got to be in the middle of your market, so that it can be sold when you're finished using it.

Erik: Corporate architecture is an area that has some icons but generally those icons are rather poor icons and not very inspiring. I think if you try to escalate this now into a fine art there aren't a lot of precedents.

Darryl: Why do we have to say it's corporate? Why is this something to confess? Why can't we just create our work? If we're taking a building type and taking it into a new expression, we're riding the edge.

*Q. How do you see Studios' responsibility to the community beyond the client?*
Gene: We want to look at what can be done rather than what has been done. I think we are able to bring the benefit of the breadth and the freedom of our thinking to some things besides just the pure artifacts, besides the pure physical surface form. It's a huge opportunity, to give design some deeper challenges. With a little more anthropological understanding, a little more sociology—understanding business drivers and how culture's changing—then we can really start to sweep through places and create environments that do involve users. Studios is the kind of place that can do that.

Charles: I see Studios' work as,

in a way, applied social science. When you're doing office work there really isn't much program there, maybe they need a hundred thousand square feet of open office, a cafeteria, truck docks. So we search for the program that is hidden within and it's done through a kind of deconstruction of what it is these people are actually doing; what is their business; what are their hopes, dreams and aspirations and how does that come out in their work. How can you take that apart and discover programs hidden within something that sounds totally generic and make an architecture out of it.

Phil: That is after all our ultimate reason for being architects. I think we have to be able to look ourselves in the mirror every morning and be able to say that what we're doing is contributing to the advancement of our society. Whether it's a better business solution or whether it's a higher art form; what it's really all about is making people feel better about what they do every day.

Q. *What's next?*
Tom: We need to bring more of ourselves and the relevance of what we feel into the work, and that might influence what kind of clients come to us next. It can go beyond the corporate dynamic, and bring a personal dynamic, an ethnic dynamic to the work. That's a different challenge that we should aspire to.

Erik: I think when we're at our best, there's this wide-eyed ability to look at a challenge without feeling too encumbered about convention or tradition. As I said, there aren't a lot of precedents for really good corporate architecture, unlike

museums or churches or performing arts centers. So it's a little like the Renaissance when the merchants developed new building typologies in Italy. We enjoy a kind of open field.

The founding principals of Studios include Darryl Roberson, FAIA, Gene Rae, Phil Olson, and Erik Sueberkrop, FAIA. Erik Sueberkrop, born in Hamburg, Germany, has been instrumental in the development of Studios' high-tech aesthetic, leading projects for SGI, Apple, 3Com and FORE Systems, and while based in the San Francisco office, has many significant projects in Europe and Asia. Phil Olson is based in the Washington D.C. office. He is strong in the development of contemporary officing strategies for law firms and corporations, with clients including Discovery Communications and Squire Sanders and Dempsey. Gene Rae is based in Washington D.C., and has concentrated on strategic planning and developing alternative officing strategies for major corporate interiors projects. Darryl Roberson, practicing since 1960, has designed over ten million square feet of high-end office space for clients as diverse as Petronas in Malaysia and AirTouch Communications in San Francisco.

Thomas Yee, AIA, graduated from the University of Michigan in 1976 and became a partner with Studios' San Francisco office in 1990. He maintains a diversified practice for clients ranging from Wilson Sonsini Goodrich & Rosati to the University of California. David Sabalvaro, AIA, joined Studios in its first year and became a partner in 1990. He has worked on projects from Apple to

Silicon Graphics, developing fast-track strategies for some of the largest and most design-intensive projects in the San Francisco office. Todd DeGarmo, AIA, divides his time between the Washington and New York offices. Partner since 1991, he has developed new office settings for clients such as Nike, Arnold and Porter, and Morgan Stanley. Bruce Skiles Danzer Jr., AIA, graduated from Harvard University before starting with Studios' Washington D.C. office, and moved to the London office as Partner-in-Charge in 1996. Specializing in innovative interiors, he has overseen numerous projects, for clients such as Hanley Wood, in the United States and Europe. Pierre Pastellas, DPLG, was born in Istanbul and joined Studios as Partner-in-Charge of the new Paris office in 1992. He has worked for European clients such as American Express Bank and Silicon Graphics in Switzerland. Charles Dilworth, AIA, named partner in 1995, graduated from Yale University in 1983 and joined Studios in 1988, working on a number of award-winning projects for a variety of clients headquartered in Silicon Valley and San Francisco. Guy Martin, AIA, was named partner in 1998. He is based in Washington D.C. and is engaged in primarily architectural projects such as Market Square North, a mixed-use office and housing project.

# The Power of the Pragmatic

*by James S. Russell, AIA*

It is rare, but a few American cities have created enormous wealth in a short time: San Francisco during the Gold Rush, Chicago in the late 19th century, Los Angeles in the 1950s. In the 1990s, the place has been Silicon Valley, where in only 40 years a matrix of companies has arisen whose combined $450 billion market value dwarfs that of Hollywood and Detroit, according to *Business Week*.

While microchips shrank, personal computers proliferated, and software got smarter, company after company spread out across the flats at the southern end of the San Francisco peninsula. Studios was there, though it wasn't a very auspicious place for architects to be. It seemed that every one of the firm's prospective clients began in someone's garage, and as they grew up they wanted to retain the nothing-to-lose fever of that startup era. They built bigger garages. Architecture seemed all but irrelevant when, for so many companies, getting hundreds of thousands of square feet

ready for occupancy as quickly as possible was struggle enough.

But these companies learned that it is hard to keep a daredevil, risk-taking culture alive once thousands, not dozens, of employees are bent to the task of finding the Next Big Thing (which, by the way, would have to be rolled out in 18 months). Apple, 3Com, Nortel, Silicon Graphics, Fore Systems—they all found in Studios a team that could actually help them think about space as a strategic resource, something that would help them get the job done better.

This is not what architecture is supposed to be. It is a high art, one intended to help our society reach its highest aspirations. But America has always been impatient with architecture as a civic, monument-building enterprise; some of the nation's key architectural contributions have been born of the marriage between architectural ambition and business necessity. Chicago architect Daniel Burnham did not invent the office building or rethink its typology. Instead he reclad the generic urban, multistory industrial loft building with an economically civic-minded expression, dressing it up so that it could take its place within the City Beautiful conception of America's elite. Burnham poured forth his unchoked and civilized vision for the filthy, chaotic American city in gorgeously pastel-hued renderings, commissioned by cities all over the country. In Detroit, Albert Kahn sculpted the most minimal bits of bolted steel into light-catching, breeze-inducing, minimalist poems of industrial necessity to fit Henry Ford's early 20th-century dream of converting raw materials to completed automobiles

within a single colossal industrial complex.

Is it fair to place Studios within this pantheon? The firm certainly deserves to be nominated. True, Studios is only one of many architectural firms that have worked in Silicon Valley. But it is only Studios that has pushed computer companies to look beyond their tendency to erect generic space. Studios does not just bring design to the unwashed code-writing masses; it delves deep into business culture. This may prove to be the firm's chief contribution: helping companies understand and express their core values, illustrating how work space can represent and support a business culture, and, in the process, redefining what architecture itself is about.

Studios is not about commercial design alone, and with offices in Washington, New York, and Paris, in addition to its home base in San Francisco, neither its outlook nor its client base is confined to Silicon Valley. But it is in the searingly competitive environment of the Valley that companies—reaping vast wealth yet assuming empire-toppling risks—may at last realize the vaunted "office of the future."

Studios has grown with its Silicon Valley clients. When projects were small and cheap, Studios learned to build client trust with pleasing (and in retrospect, obvious) solutions to easily overlooked office problems. At Apple Computer's 1986 Advanced Computer Technology Center, for example, a lavender-painted cable tray slips above rows of office workstations, curling up at the end and sliding away under the ceiling. The simple placement of utilitarian cable trays in a convenient location encouraged software

engineers to rewire at will, and also proved esthetically elegant.

The typical high-growth company's first instinct is to build raw space, as much of it as unencumbered as possible. The windowless warehouse of cast-on-site, tilted-into-place concrete may be fast and cheap, but it is also the most amenity-free form of quickly-tenanted space—the closest thing to a garage. Studios has helped its clients see that people can't work productively for long in such raw space: they need light, a connection to what's going on in the rest of the world, and places for interaction and relaxation.

Northern Telecom (Nortel), the Canadian telecommunications company, asked Studios to help their R & D and manufacturing sides work more collaboratively together. The architect's key move was to take three dreary warehouses attached to each other and rip a giant S-shaped corridor out of the middle of them. The corridor creates a generous common "street," where various departments have the opportunity to see what others are doing. It thrusts out of the existing building envelope in a metal-framed prow, letting the visitor know where the entrance is, but also announcing that this isn't the same old anonymous Valley workplace. The architects dropped a skylit atrium into the middle of the complex to create the equivalent of a town square. Most of the time groups of Nortel staff can assemble for informal meetings simply by pushing tables and chairs together, but to celebrate a product rollout or to relay important company news, the space can be made into a big auditorium. Though it is constructed of spec-budget miscellaneous metal

and drywall, it is a monumentally sculptural space, one of the most satisfying the firm has made. More important, the firm created a much richer workplace environment out of raw material that seemed to offer little promise.

Many clients finally traded up from concrete walls and ceilings hung with sagging batts of plastic-faced insulation to the speculative-office standard of metal decking, steel columns, and bar joists. Such buildings were inexpensive, but they could be more readily tweaked.

At 3Com's corporate headquarters, Studios added two buildings to an existing campus of speculative structures. While the design picks up cues from the existing buildings, the designers made architectural events out of entrances, stairs, canopies, a fitness center, and other "public" functions. The spaces duplicate the ballet of the everyday on the streets of a city, where people see and are seen, where they schmooze, where they catch up on each other's lives and work. Of course, such informal interaction is part of the agenda of companies like 3Com, which count on accidental encounters to spark the creative juices that make great things happen.

"We need 150,000 square feet in 12 months," the fast-growing client might explain. "Oh, and we have no idea who will be in it, or even if we will still need it by then—or if we will need more." These are not problems amenable to the usual blocking and stacking diagrams drawn by the corporate space planner. For companies riding a wave of heady but treacherous megagrowth, the act of building can uncover deep fissures in company identity and culture. More and more companies

find themselves betting very large numbers of people and a great deal of money on unproved ideas—and then doing it again. When the product mix or deployment of resources is radically changed every two years or so, should CEOs not ask themselves what is fundamental about the company they run? Architecture need not impede perpetual corporate transformation. It can actually expresses the fundamental values and purpose of the company, though this is a far more daunting task for architects than detailing an elegant curtain wall or coming up with a drop-dead lobby. It asks the practitioner to participate in a far deeper dialogue during the design, and to deliver not just space, but something akin to an armature for change.

The 1994 Shoreline Entry Site for Silicon Graphics signaled the first real departure from the Valley's reflective-glass anonymity, and led the way to a series of projects that began to express architecturally a sociology of work. The exterior of the building for the first time became much more sculptural, acting as a billboard and recruitment poster. It offers a long, sweeping curve to the freeway, punctuated by an oversize, arching entrance canopy. In plan it appears as if the usual large, pancake-like floor plate has been pulled apart. At this "fissure," the firm installed stairs, meeting places, coffee bars, and other such collaboration-inducing amenities. High ceilings and external circulation created a more amenable workplace by making daylight and views part of the everyday experience of the otherwise cubicle-bound worker.

As Studios' clients moved on to building half-million-square-foot campuses from scratch, the stakes—

and the opportunities—rose. Studios describes Silicon Graphics' North Charleston campus as a kind of high-tech hilltown. Its ponds, pools, walkways, towers, and pavilions, shot through here and there with second-level futuristic-looking bridges, create an unforgettable environmental identity. But there is an agenda behind the eye-catching architectural gestures and the diverse palette of materials: Silicon Graphics has reached a size at which maintaining loyalty, solidarity, and a focus on corporate goals becomes ever more difficult, especially for a company that must meld engineering, manufacturing, and creative cultures. Individual buildings cluster around a central landscaped courtyard, with entrances, stairs, and other common spaces housed in transparent, winglike appendages. Bridges and internal pedestrian spines become an armature to which are attached deep, amorphous, floor plates for both engineering and manufacturing. Dining and other common activities take place in separate buildings so that people have opportunities to traverse and use the rich variety of social spaces provided. The prominence of circulation makes the idea of moving from one building to another more important, thereby encouraging curiosity about activity outside the workers' own realm. With most parking banished to a podium stretching under the buildings, it was possible to augment the complex with lush courtyards and landscaping.

Silicon Valley is not the whole story of Studios, and the design-for-perpetual-change ethos that works so well for Bay Area firms increasingly applies to clients ranging from white-shoe law firms to blue-chip

corporations. Lawyers at Washington's Arnold & Porter law firm found themselves increasingly isolated from each other as on-line research usurped the collegial atmosphere of the law library. Inserting a multifloor atrium into the spec-building envelope and creating a "garden room" for after-work socializing were among the ways Studios used architecture to restore a sense of connection to the firm's 1,000-plus staff.

AirTouch sought to stay connected to its well-regarded roots as one of the "Baby Bell" telephone companies while navigating the high-risk shoals of wireless telecommunications. Studios fostered a more entrepreneurial environment in the company's downtown high-rise environment by maintaining easy physical movement from floor to floor. Locating the main reception area, conference rooms, and other commonly used services on an elevator-transfer floor (where everyone has to stop), the architects created the corporate equivalent of a central square.

Miami's Discovery Channel shared the Silicon Valley dilemma of rapid growth while trying to maintain a reputation for high-quality programming. Here, the task was a balancing act, since an environment that enables creativity is not necessarily one that is assertively creative-looking. The work area layouts are particularly intriguing in their casual arrangement of conventional office furniture and nicely designed plywood storage dividers; there is plenty of "design" at Discovery, but also plenty of opportunity for people to reinterpret the space to suit their work.

Hanley-Wood, a Washington magazine publisher, breaks down walls that other publishers find

insurmountable. To restructure operations flexibly and spin off new publications (electronic and print), Hanley-Wood blurred the lines between publications and placed key shared resources around a skylit atrium. The company principals also wanted to make themselves more accessible to staff; exterior offices are correspondingly more transparent and less private.

There are subtle, if not subversive, inversions of architectural tradition in what Studios does. Architects often use materials—stone, masonry, wood paneling—to denote hierarchy or specify difference. But in today's business environment, the hierarchies are played down; the awe-inspring lobby and the hushed, isolated corner office are taboo. Studios uses spatial drama and architectural materials in a much different way: to signal the youthful, no-holds-barred nature of the workplace, to serve as a recruitment billboard, and to recognize the unhierarchical nature of the space. In this topsy-turvy work world, the fitness center or coffee bar gets the most lavish architectural attention.

Another inversion brings the idea of the city inside the building. Today's freeway-webbed office-park realm is an urban environment without the trappings of a city. Parking-swathed buildings, none of which has any but the most tenuous relationship with its surroundings, lack the communal social and economic activity that streets provide. But Studios has found the potential for rich life in this fluourescent-lit, reflective-glass cocoon. They build internalized equivalents of the city—streets, avenues, plazas, parks and gardens, and civic and commercial functions—

within the 60,000 to 100,000 square feet enclosed by the typical spec building. As the firm has attracted more institutional clients, they have enriched the metaphor. The design for Paris' Société Générale incorporates rotundas linking axial corridors, a miniature of Haussman's design for the entire city.

The third inversion is impermanence. The lifespan of many of Studios' environments can be measured in a handful of years; the idea of a building that might go without significant alteration for 15 years or more is for some clients unimaginable. Such circumstances provide no place for permanent materials or "timeless" design. Yet architects are trained to think of their work as potentially timeless, as superseding style. Studios' designs are open-ended, adaptable and accepting of change. In this they are the heirs to a noble lineage, one that shares the adaptability of the humble "temporary" buildings at MIT (praised by Whole Earth pioneer Stewart Brand in his influential *How Buildings Learn*) and the esthetic power of the vast industrial sheds built by Albert Kahn for the automotive industry in its golden age.

Can buildings of the highest order be made of such ingredients? The question has often bedeviled American architecture. To place Studios in the canon of great business architects, such as Albert Kahn or Daniel Burnham, is high praise indeed, but architecture with a capital A is not what many of today's business clients need. Those of us who think that architecture is important want it to aspire to something more than just elegant pragmatic solutions.

It should say something about a place and its users, and it should speak to the future. Studios has had few opportunities to do architecture on this level, and clients' tendency to pigeonhole architects will make it an uphill climb for the firm to translate its few important institutional projects, such as the Shanghai Opera House and the University of California, Davis, Alumni Building, into a body of work made outside the corporate pressure cooker.

But by being so deeply involved with businesses struggling to manage change, the firm is poised to make what may become the key architectural development of our time: design that can support institutional change on a scale and in ways we cannot yet imagine. From software to advertising to management consulting, businesses are already finding that they can't change quickly enough, that today's perpetual "re-orgs" don't take deeply or fast enough, that no one yet knows how to implement flexible business structures across large organizations. According to the received wisdom, architecture has nothing to do with this. Studios is in a position to prove that it does, which would represent a breakthrough of historic proportions.

Studios' synthetic vision convinces me that they can make whatever leaps they choose. Certainly they are acquainted with what few architectural verities are left in an age that seems to have little use for this ancient art. That they can get some urbaneness and some architectural amenity into projects that traditionally have had no architectural nature at all is testimony to the fundamentally humanistic outlook that any architect needs to be great.

# Works

# Apple Computer
# Various Interiors
## Cupertino, California 1986-93

Apple Computer was born in co-founder Steve Wozniak's garage, and despite its phenomenal growth in the 1980's, it has held firmly to its casual roots. Intensive improvement of its facilities—a score of speculative office and industrial buildings leased in suburban Silicon Valley—reinforced the company's image.

The Advanced Computer Technology Center (ACTC) was Studios' 1986 breakthrough design project for Apple. In its 22,000-square-foot interior, the architects synthesized elemental, tectonic forms with unorthodox material applications and a bold color palette. Sine-wave "roofs" over offices are part of a highly innovative design executed with simple materials such as drywall, aluminum-framed windows, and hollow-core doors. The Cray, then the fastest commercial computer in the world, was incorporated into the design in a place of prominence, behind a large window on a viewing platform within a square, purple-painted chamber. The room where it sits was positioned to bisect the black-and-white-tiled, gable-roofed central corridor, the termination of which was underscored with a bright red wall. Beyond this centerpiece, the architects devoted the building to workspaces that would coexist with machinery.

Workstations for the engineers, who work at computers linked to the Cray, became the focal point of the ACTC design. Here Studios created a two-inch wiring chase within the inner walls of the stations along with an overhead network of open cable trays. The overhead trays were painted lavender and connected to the indirect lighting system to become part of the total design vocabulary. While the plan called for an open office layout, divided by a central corridor, the architects established some freestanding forms within the space to host conference rooms, two private offices, and rest rooms. Studios Architecture designed Apple Computer's ACTC facility as a visual celebration of technology, and much of the architectural vocabulary established here was later applied to other quick, modestly-budgeted projects for Apple.

The architects located the corporate Fitness Center in an adjacent 22,000 square-foot, tilt-up, windowless concrete warehouse; here they continued to use playful, geometric language and unconventional materials.

For Apple's Learning Center, an 82,500-square-foot employee training and continuing education facility, the architects established a double-height central break-out space that became the setting for several architectural pavilions. Occupied in 1990, the facility was designed to accommodate up to 500 users simultaneously in sixteen classrooms. The break-out space also provides public and private phones and an e-mail center.

By 1992, Apple was ready to build an 856,000-square-foot Research & Development Campus, a facility that would carry the company into the future. The exterior architecture of the campus would be unified, while the interior of each of its six buildings was to be unique; to ensure this, different architects were selected for each interior design project, with Studios designing Buildings Two and Five.

For the research facilities, Apple required 85% enclosed offices, a departure from their typical open-cubicle environment. To lure the engineers out of their potentially isolating workplaces, the architects created several living-room-like areas on each floor, spontaneous, interactive work areas with coffee, sofas, and white boards. To make the user-defined areas comfortable, the designers lowered the ceiling by floating a canopy and arranged the furniture in residential configurations.

Opening page,
view of the access
corridor ACTC.

Above, the ACTC
circulation hub.

Right, ACTC
axonometric.

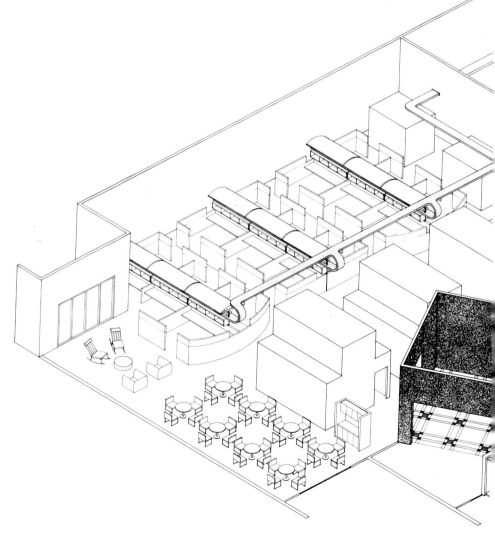

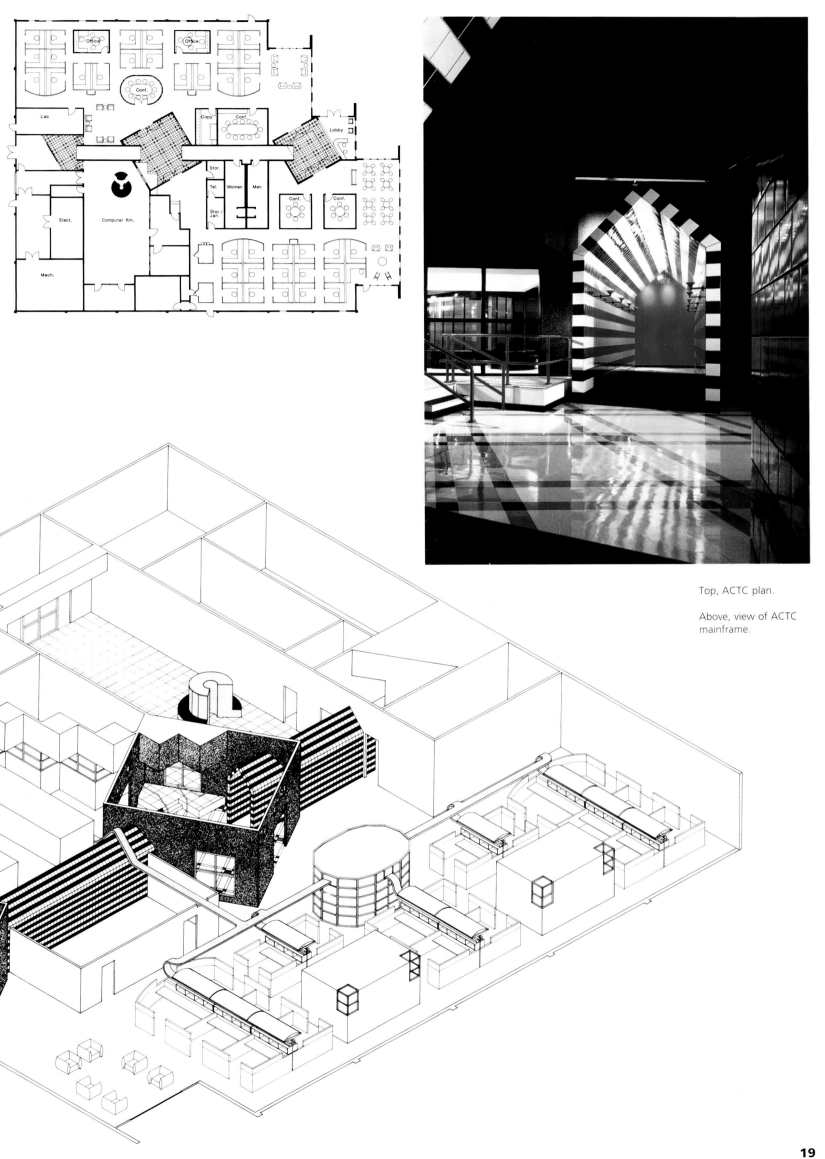

Top, ACTC plan.

Above, view of ACTC mainframe.

Below, ACTC detail
of a workstation.

Right, ACTC cable tray.

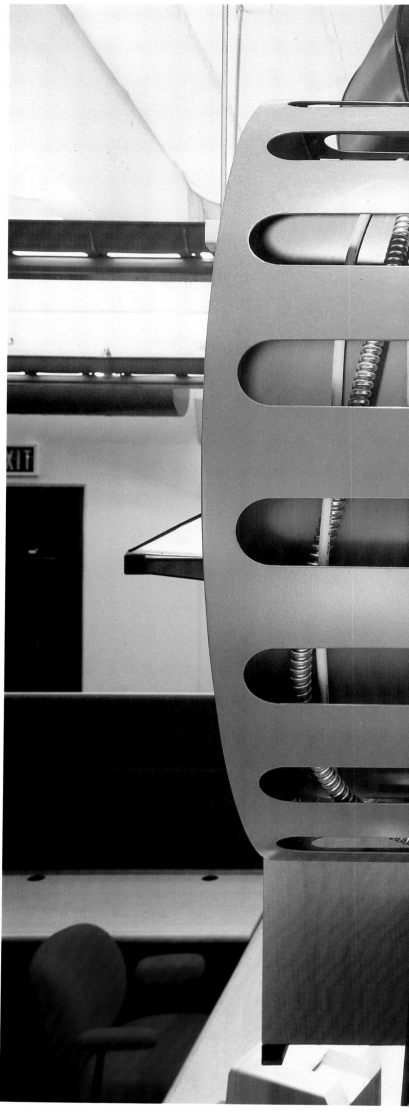

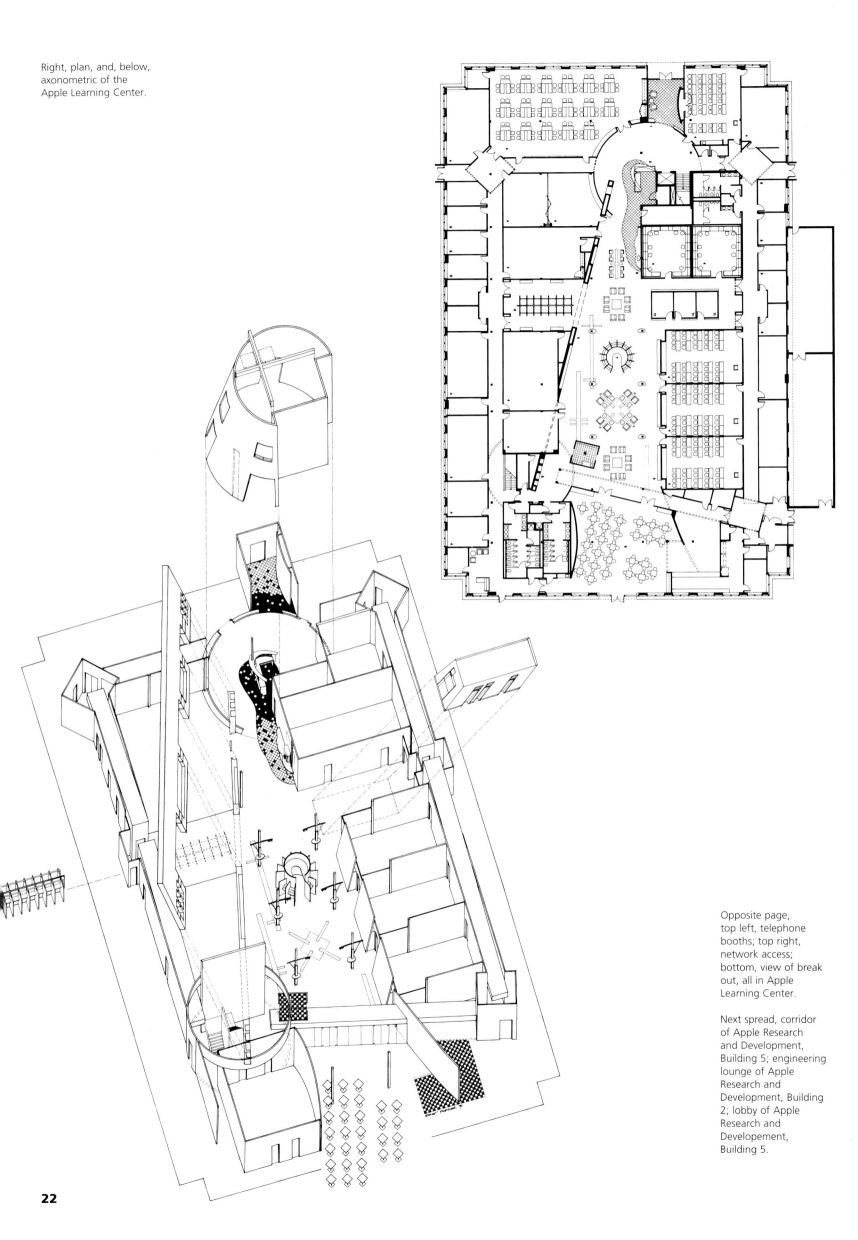

Right, plan, and, below,
axonometric of the
Apple Learning Center.

Opposite page,
top left, telephone
booths; top right,
network access;
bottom, view of break
out, all in Apple
Learning Center.

Next spread, corridor
of Apple Research
and Development,
Building 5; engineering
lounge of Apple
Research and
Development, Building
2; lobby of Apple
Research and
Developement,
Building 5.

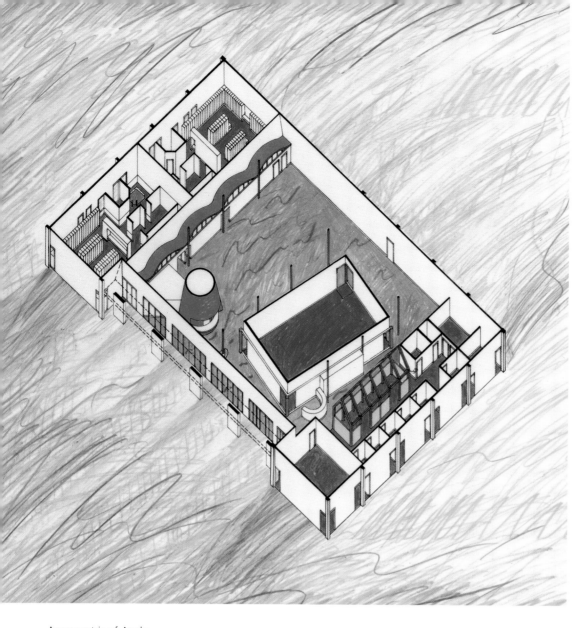

Axonometric of Apple
Fitness Center.

Opposite page, entry
and aerobics room
of Apple Fitness Center.

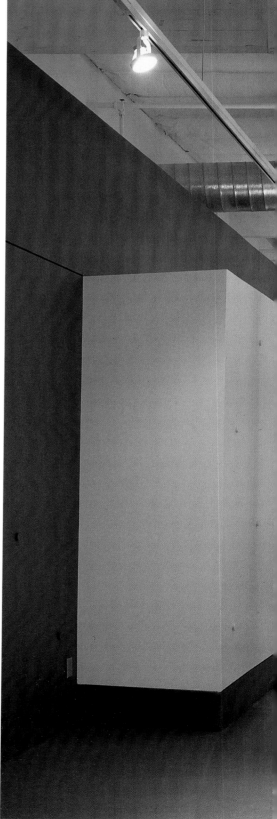

Staff area of Apple
Fitness Center.

# Silicon Graphics, Inc.
# Various Interiors
## Mountain View, California 1988-96

Studios Architecture designed several tenant improvements for Silicon Graphics' headquarters, a 600,000-square-foot complex of existing brick-clad tilt-up concrete structures. A progressive and open minded client, Silicon Graphics allowed the architects to experiment with these environments, defined mostly by manipulations of drywall and paint.

Building 8, completed in 1988, is the first of these projects. It is distinguished by a monumental stairway surrounded by a double height rotunda connecting all functions. In contrast to the traditional separation of manufacturing and engineering divisions (with the former typically given back-room status), Studios put them both in one facility here, in keeping with the client's specific programmatic requirement. Silicon Graphics' egalitarian philosophy encouraged the architects not only to celebrate the manufacturing process as the core of the business, but also to create a design that would encourage interaction between the manufacturing and engineering staff, facilitating collaboration and innovation.

The Systems Software division, located in Building 9 and completed in 1990, is designed as a metaphor of a city. The architects established primary circulation paths, or "boulevards," to connect the front and back of the 62,000-square-foot building. Stairs at the terminus of each of the four boulevards eliminate the need for costly, fire-rated corridors. Secondary "streets" were then established to link neighborhoods of engineering office clusters to the primary paths. An open area at the core "central park" takes on a more organic expression: the leaning walls and exposed metal studs of the blue-green plaster structure which contain the coffee, copy, and rest room facilities were designed to suggest natural forms.

The Product Demonstration Center, located in Building 6, was completed in 1992. Functioning primarily as a high profile facility for potential customers, the space is also occupied by senior executives. The design communicates an image of the human transformed by technology and technology informed by the human. The focal point of the entrance is a spiral stair coiled around a vertical triangular truss, with computer monitors creating a "technology tower" leading to demo and briefing areas on the second floor.

Studios also designed an environment for the engineering group at Silicon Studio, a pioneer division of Silicon Graphics focusing on digital entertainment and multimedia. The objective in this off-site, 100,000-square-foot warehouse was to design an environment that would reflect and encourage the group's experimental energy.

Opening page,
view of stair of the
Customer Briefing
Center at Silicon
Graphics Building 6.

Right, plan of Silicon
Graphics Building 9.

Below, axonometric
of Silicon Graphics
Building 8.

Opposite page,
axonometric of Silicon
Graphics Building 9.

Next spread, left, views
to and of entry and
central stair of Silicon
Graphics Building 8;
right, engineering
lounge of Silicon
Graphics Building 9.

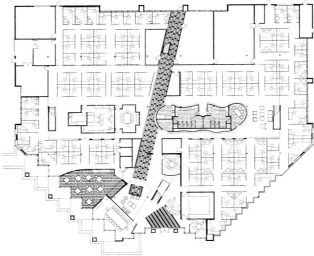

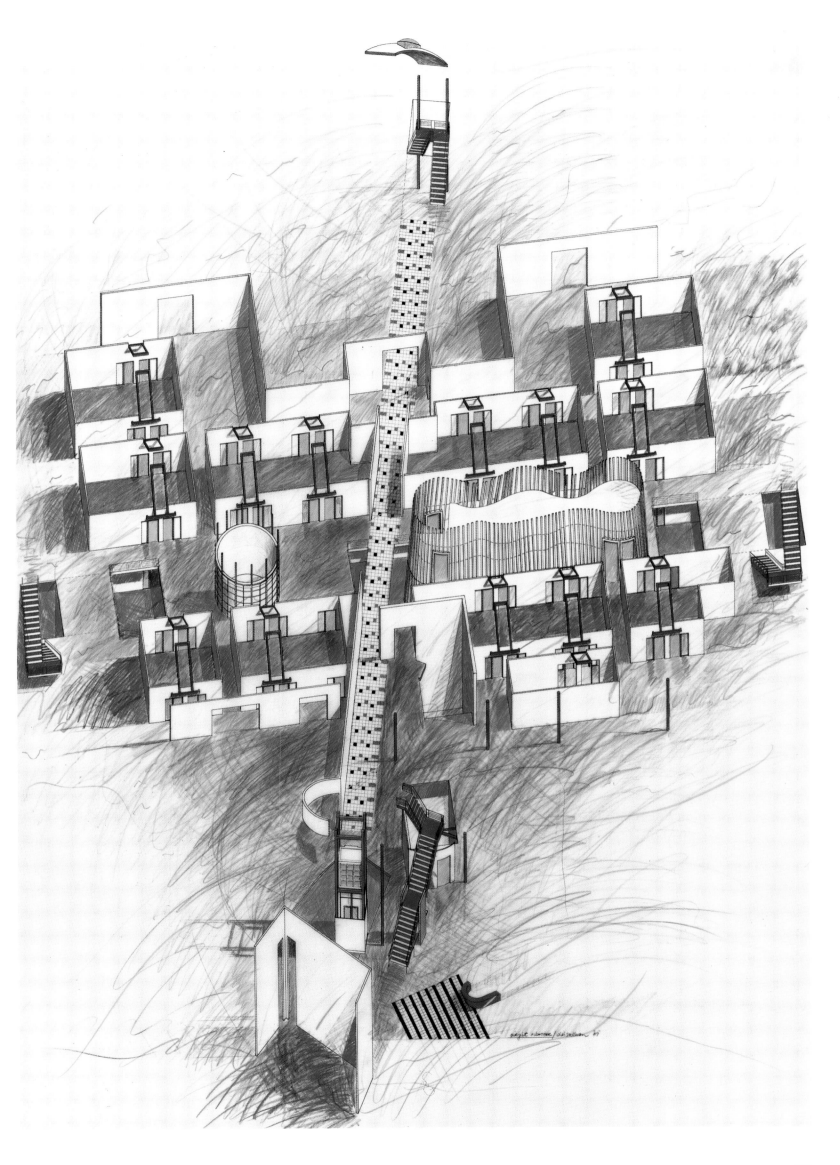

Elevator at entry, and below, central bathroom core of Silicon Graphics Building 9.

Left, cable tray and circulation of Silicon Graphics Building 9.

Opposite page, break area of Silicon Studio.

Corridor and, right,
view of offices
of Silicon Studio.

Below, floor plan
of Silicon Studio.

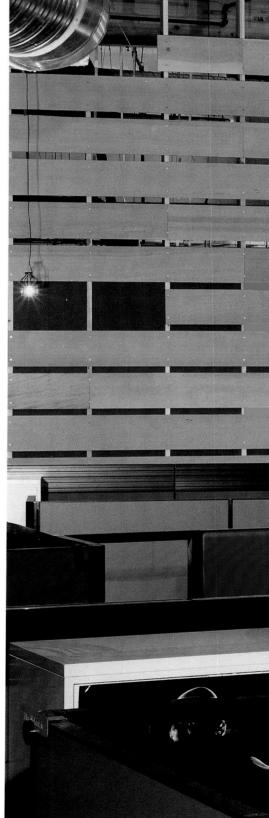

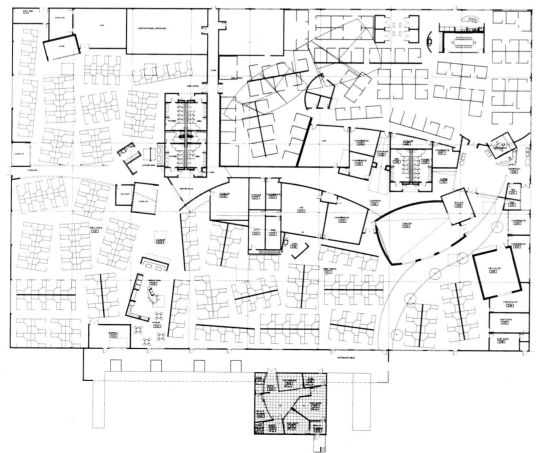

# 3Com Corporation Headquarters
## Santa Clara, California 1990-99

3Com, the world's second-largest maker of computer networking equipment, has been incrementally expanding its corporate headquarters over the past decade, according to a master plan developed by Studios in 1988. The original four-building, 500,000-square-foot complex is located amid nondescript industrial development alongside a busy highway.

The second phase of construction consists of two buildings totaling 375,000 square feet. As in the first phase, the majority of the space is for manufacturing, research and development, but also includes a 12,000-square-foot fitness center, a 120-seat dining facility, a customer briefing center, and a training facility. The massing derives from interlocking volumes and plan rotations that respond to and reconcile various geometries established in the previous phase. The use of the profiled metal panels and EIFS cladding are also derivative of the pre-existing campus context. As the project assumed greater density, with parking structures replacing surface lots, it became necessary to create paved pedestrian zones connecting various functions campus-wide. To soften what grew into a relatively urban landscape, the architects added a reflecting pond, which doubles as a secondary water supply for the new manufacturing building.

When 3Com outgrew the site, it procured a twelve-acre parcel immediately to the east (Phase III), across a seasonal drainage creek. The architects discovered that the two sites could be well integrated by building atop a level parking podium covering a large percentage of the new site. Four buildings comprising 537,000 square feet were designed for engineering, a corporate data center, and a third cafeteria. The new construction will be arranged around a landscaped courtyard, with a 300 foot long pedestrian bridge connecting this phase, currently under construction, to the existing buildings.

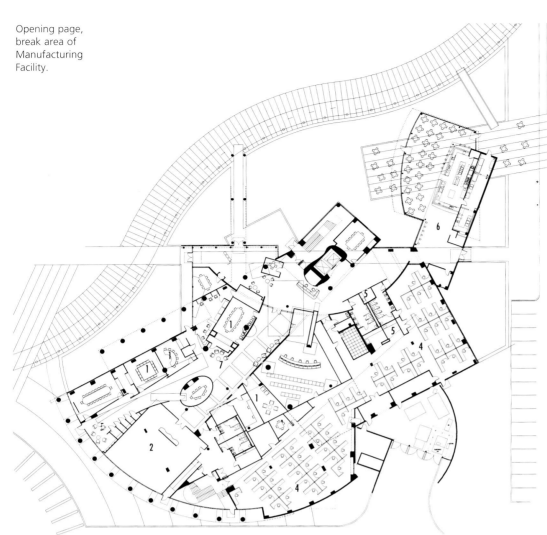

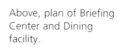

Above, plan of Briefing
Center and Dining
facility.

Below, east elevation
of Training and
Manufacturing Facility.

Right, Manufacturing Neighborhood Center.

Below, Training and Fitness Center.

Opposite page, top, "Town Center" exterior between Dining and Fitness and Training Centers; bottom, entrance to Briefing Center and Manufacturing Component.

Below, plan of Manufacturing and Fitness Center.

Bottom, dining facility.

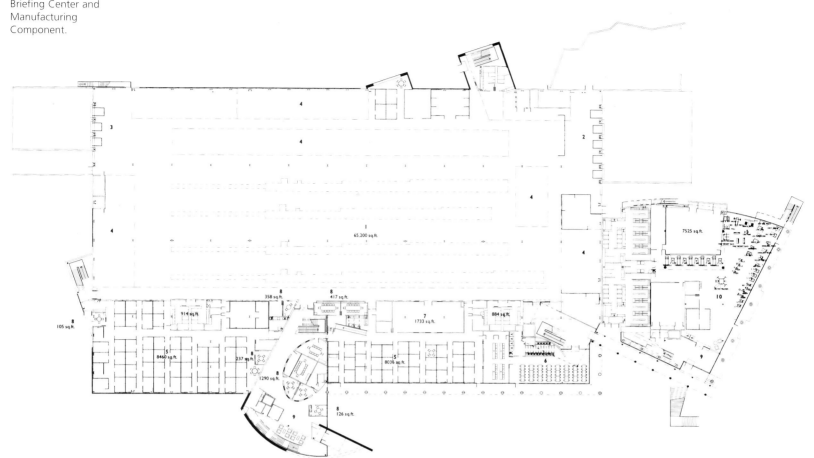

Opposite page, lobby at
Manufacturing.

Right, plan of Phase III.

Below, model looking
south at Phase III.

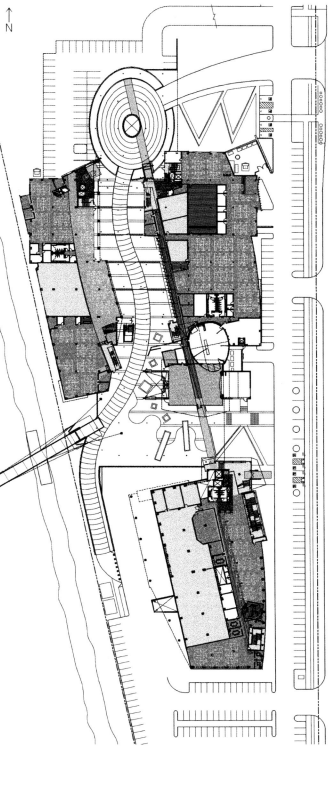

# University of California, Davis Alumni & Visitors Center
## Davis, California 1992

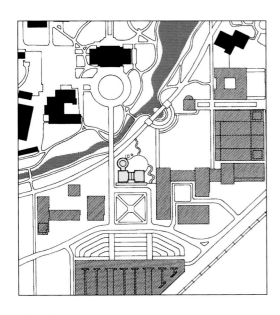

Opposite page, entry arcade; above, site plan; below, view from the Arboretum.

The Alumni and Visitors Center was the first major project to be executed in the University's master plan for its southern expansion. On a site highly visible from the freeway, it would unite the Alumni Association, Career Recruiting, international visitors, and campus tours offices. The architects saw the importance of establishing a strong presence with the Center, and designed the 21,000 square foot facility as the gateway to both the campus and to the Southern expansion.

The imposing symmetry of two simple wings flanking a three-story tower creates a bold first impression for visitors to the campus. For this relatively small building the architects created an expression of monumentality more commonly associated with civic architecture. The design incorporated a masonry and timber arcade to provide a human scale to the entry sequence and to refer to the University's agricultural roots.

The rear of the building represents a relaxed departure from the formality of the facade. An octagonal special programs room anchors the prominent corner location while sheltering a landscaped courtyard from the street. Inspired by the natural environment of the adjacent Learning Arboretum and Putah Creek, the architects created an intimate indoor-outdoor setting for conferences, exhibitions, and alumni events.

The airy, light-filled atrium in the gable-roofed tower is the building's interior focus; expressive steel scissors trusses pull the eye upward and provide instant appreciation for the open spaces. Fluid overlapping of functional zones on the ground level create flexible uses for large groups while maximizing useable space.

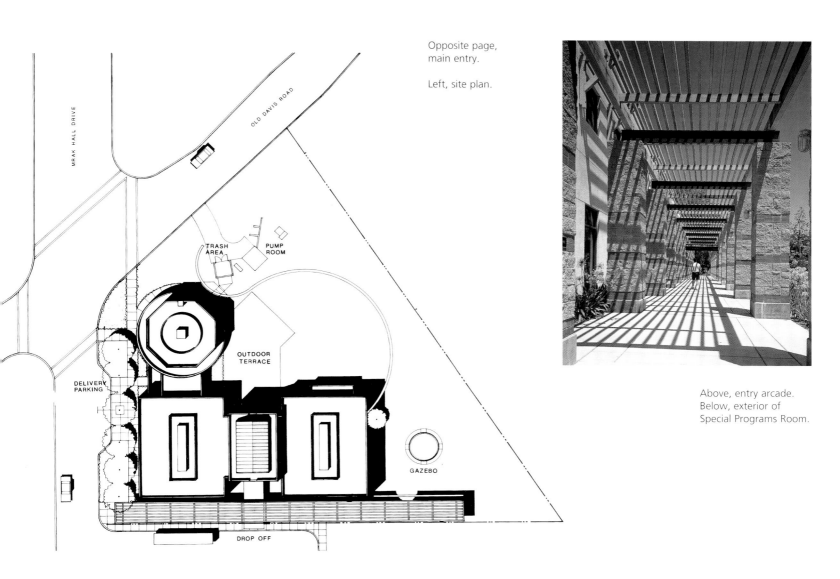

Opposite page,
main entry.

Left, site plan.

Above, entry arcade.
Below, exterior of
Special Programs Room.

Opposite page,
reception lobby.
Below, plan of the
ground floor.

Right, plan of the
second floor.

Bottom, interior
of Special Programs
Room.

# Knoll International GmbH Showroom
## Frankfurt, Germany 1992

The 7,000 square foot furniture showroom is located on the ground floor of an existing building along the tree lined east bank of the Main River in Frankfurt, Germany. Studios designed a retail space that focuses attention on the Knoll Group's products while upholding the sophisticated architectural context of the surrounding museum district.

The design creates a naturalistic environment using the elemental materials (unfinished wood, glass, and metals) and geometries (circle and square) of furniture design. Running across the back of the showroom is a screen of 40cm x 40cm rough spruce timbers. The primitive, tressel like construction has an understated power that balances expressive design and pragmatic function. A visual counterpoint to the display space, the screen permits views through the exhibition area while providing a physical boundary for the office space behind.

Additional private offices were created with parallel metal and glass panels suspended from an overhead steel armature. Varying degrees of transparency and privacy are achieved through use of the adjustable and pivoting perforated screens. Perforated metal is also employed, curved and stained, in the conference room ceiling on the opposite side of the reception hall.

The showroom's color and material palette is subdued and natural. The architects took full advantage of the abundant natural light coming through the storefront, and kept all product lighting sources to an understated minimum. The result is a quiet yet powerful setting for the artful display of goods and transaction of commerce; Studios' design exemplifies the Knoll credo, "Good Design is Good Business."

Opposite page, the showroom.

Below, isometric from Main River.

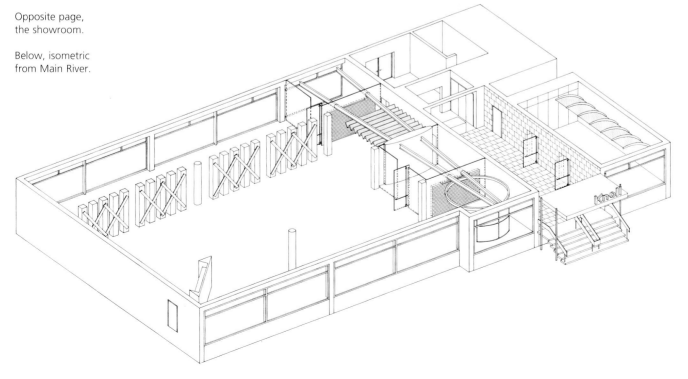

Below,
open office area.

Bottom, pivoting
perforated screen.

Left, view from
Main River and access
road.

Below, view from
showroom back
to entry.

# Varet Marcus & Fink
## Washington D.C. 1992

In responding to Varet Marcus & Fink's desire to be "more than just another Washington law firm," the critical challenges were to make very efficient use of the available space while giving a small firm a larger presence and capitalizing on spectacular views.

The design is ordered by two pairs of converging walls that meet in a reception "rotunda." One pair of converging walls extends from the elevator lobby and connects a conference room to the south and the library to the north. From the reception area, a second pair of walls extends to the west window-wall and encloses the main conference room. Each architectural feature is designated by a different construction and finish.

The lobby/library walls pair a massive wall of pale ochre plaster with a wall assembled of mahogany panels, aluminum fins, and rotary brushed stainless steel panels, the former giving the sense of a solid, pre-existing structure while the latter refers to the ground floor building lobby. The reception/conference room walls of painted drywall and bleached movingue reinforce the natural light from perimeter windows and indicate the transition to the more functional areas of the law firm. The four walls intersect the reception area, a cylinder of deeply tinted blue plaster.

Whereas the architecture of the lobby, conference, and reception areas explore forced perspectives via the illusory qualities of richly grained wood, brushed steel and waxed plaster, the architecture of the attorney areas is ordered, rhythmic and less elaborate in the use of materials. Along the west wall of the building, each structural bay is sub-divided into a pair of attorney offices and a pair of secretarial stations. The architecture is one of open, well-lit working areas that reflect the importance of the team working relationships and direct flow of work amongst attorneys and secretaries.

While considerable attention was given to efficiently accommodating Varet Marcus & Fink's program and to the complex interplay of geometry and materials, the overriding design intent was to bring a fresh perspective to the building architecture and to retain the "penthouse" quality of the building's top floor.

Opposite page, view through attorney support area.

Below, floorplan.

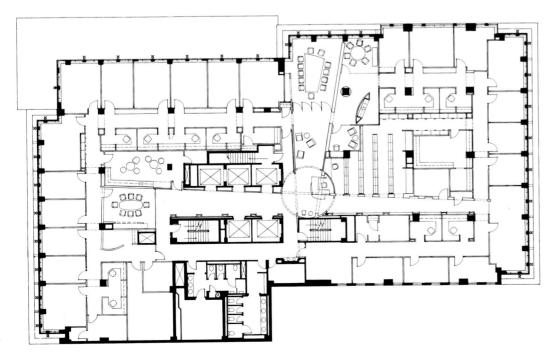

Below, the conference room and view through attorney support area.

Opposite page, corridor adjacent to conference room; below, Reception Rotunda.

# 3Com Corporation
## Dublin, Ireland 1992-1997

This multi-phased manufacturing complex is located north of Dublin, in a suburban industrial park bordering verdant Irish farmland. For Studios Architecture, the primary design challenge was to create human scale within the enormous, boxy buildings required for the manufacturing process. Their design strategy separated the functional program into discrete elements, then manipulated them into a "village" of smaller scale structure; the manufacturing buildings became backdrops that fade into the often gray Irish sky.

The design refers to the components of the medieval Irish castle: tower, keep, and moat. The first phase, 120,000 square foot building was positioned on axis with the primary vehicular artery into the park, creating a front-only exposure. Against this long, metal clad wall, the entry cone, vaulted dining room, and reflecting pond create a strong, minimalist composition.

Like 3Com at Santa Clara, the Dublin facility is a hybrid structure, both a factory and an office. In Dublin, however, the factory function is likely to grow, whereas the office function is not. The relatively stable functions, including offices and cafeteria are situated at the front end, in an area designed like a high tech sculpture, to lend the company a strong public image. The back of the building extends in a long line to optimize the manufacturing layout and was designed to be expandable. It is constructed as a plain, corrugated metal box ready to extend further as needed.

The second phase consisted of another 120,000 square foot manufacturing structure and a three story, 40,000-square-foot research and development building. Ground face concrete unit masonry with horizontal bands of engineering brick was used on the office building, as well as on a tapered entry tower (part of manufacturing) that echoes the Phase One cone. A substantially enlarged dining facility with a fan-like metal roof erupts from ground level. The two phases are united by a glass enclosed pedestrian link paralleling the pond. With large scale manufacturing and distribution facilities master planned for the northern reaches of the site, the new courtyard, defined by buildings of varying form and material, serves as the social center of the complex.

Opposite page, Dining Facility looking to Phase I Training Room and Entry Cone.

Below, site plan.

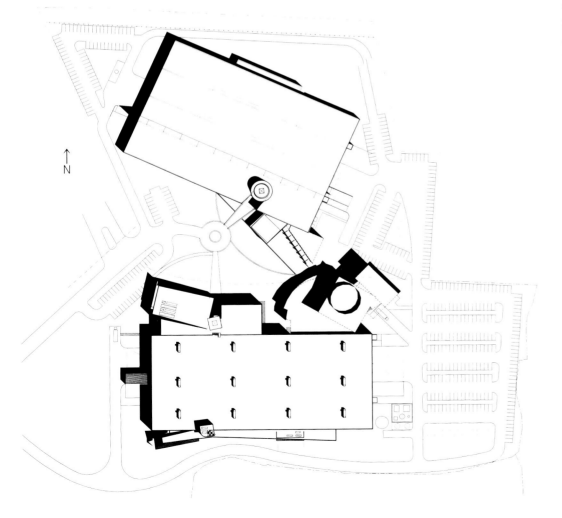

N

Opposite page, top, Phase I Entry Cone; bottom, Dining Facility with three-story Research and Development Building beyond.

Above, Entry Cone exterior.

Right, Entry Cone interior.

# Apple Computer United Kingdom
## London, England 1993

Apple Europe and Apple United Kingdom, two distinct corporate divisions, commissioned Studios to design research, training, and conference facilities in an existing 60,000 square foot building in Stockley Park, Britain's most prestigious business park. Some of Apple Europe's departments, previously based in Paris, ware the primary tenant, but several U.K. departments were mixed in for balance. Partly in response to the understated, elegant interiors of the adjacent U.K. headquarters, Apple requested a livelier environment in the new building.

The company wanted to reinforce a working creative community by drawing employees together and harnessing the ideas that arise from-on site chance encounters and physical proximity. In the three story atrium at the heart of the building, Studios created a vertical "town square," an area providing circulation, meeting, and social space, as well as service offices for managers and leaders. Lounge areas located on each floor contain coffee, vending machines, and mail boxes, and encourage informal gatherings around the atrium.

At the base of the atrium, the main entrance presents visitors with architectural elements surrounding and penetrating the multi-level space. A glass partition, supported by vertical stainless steel trusses, secures a confidential area from the public on the ground floor; it is interrupted by a polished masonry conference tower rising three stories. The main staircase pierces a glass block wall that visually screens the library. The architects also designed an all glass pedestrian link to define the new facility's main entrance while connecting it to the existing headquarters. The structurally glazed roof and suspended glass walls provide protection from the elements with maximum transparency.

Opposite page, pedestrian link.

Below, plan of the ground floor.

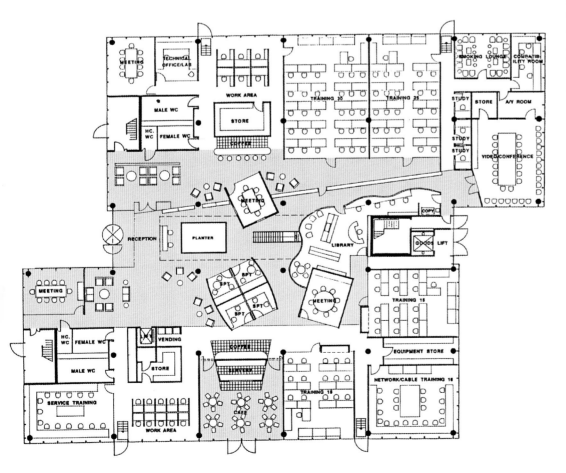

Below, detail of the
glass partition.

Left, exterior view of link.

Below, main level training area.

# Silicon Graphics, Inc.
# Shoreline Entry Site Building
## Mountain View, California  1994

Silicon Graphics clearly communicated to Studios Architecture that they wanted this building, their first in the United States, to be a strong architectural presence, and not just another Silicon Valley high-tech facility. Silicon Graphics selected a highly visible site along heavily-traveled Highway 101 so that the building would be seen daily by thousands of commuters. The city of Mountain View and the client requested that Studios create a building that would function as a gateway:  the local planning board hoped the building would mark the entry to this developing, high-tech neighborhood, while Silicon Graphics wanted the building to act as a billboard, identifying the beginning of their corporate campus.

Silicon Graphics is an aggressive, advanced-technology company that thrives on creativity and play. "One of our primary markets and the founding purpose of our company is graphic visualization, so, you should expect us to make a visual impact with our architecture," said Ray Johnson, Vice President of Corporate Facilities for Silicon Graphics. "We're anything but conventional, and our buildings should be the same". Departing from the reflective glass anonymity typical of Silicon Valley structures, the architects appropriated a computer graphics aesthetic and translated it into physical structure, with hooking arcs, layers of transparent planes, and three dimensional metal grids on the facade.

The design of the two story, 111,600-square-foot building took its cues from the sweeping energy and speed of the nearby freeway. The broad curve of the street facade decelerates in mass and scale as it moves toward the vehicular entry. The transition to human scale is marked by a huge pre-existing ash tree that presides over the visitor parking area and the suspended, thrusting canopy of the porte cochere. The plan, a simple rectangle eroded by two courtyards, one peripheral and one central, is overlaid by a linear circulation spine, connecting the stair and service cores. The cleaving effects of the spine and the courtyard divide the massing into three primary elements.

Opposite page,
the bay window
on the south facade.

Below, site plan.

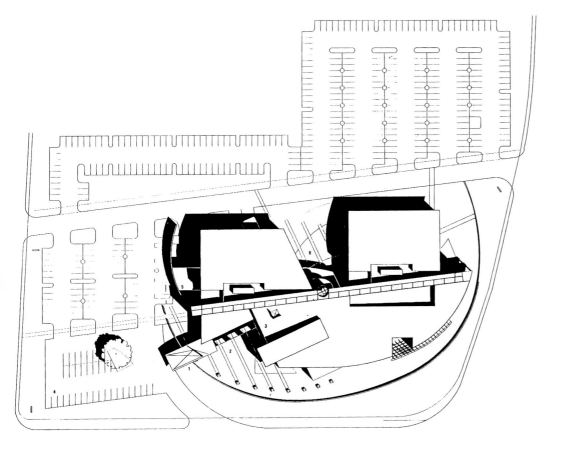

The south entry.

Below, plan of the
ground floor.

Bottom, the south
facade.

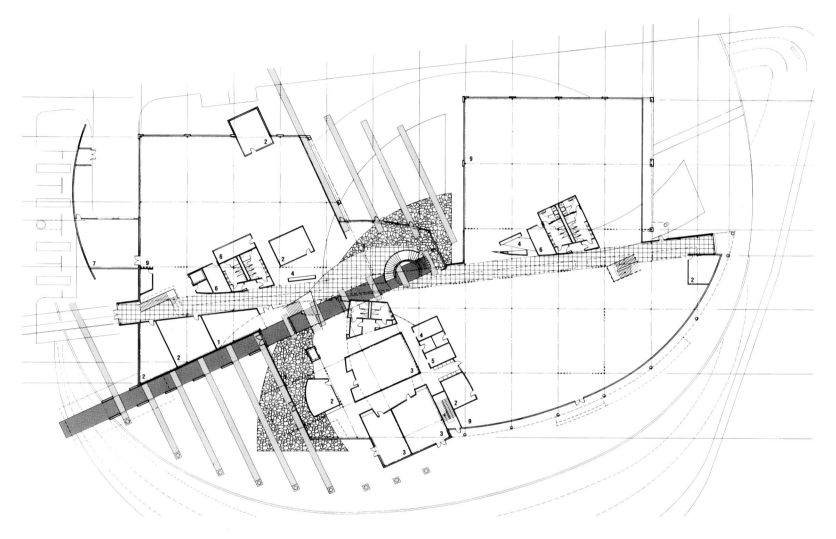

Main entry.

Entry court.

Above, view of lobby.

Below, view of offices.

Left, plan of the second floor with expansion.

Opposite page, circulation hub and dining.

# International Trade Mart
## Osaka, Japan 1994

The 2.1 million square foot International Trade Mart is part of the Asia and Pacific Trade Center, the largest showcase for foreign products in the world. The mission of the Center is to provide easier access to Japanese markets, enabling companies to bypass the multi-tiered Japanese distribution system and sell directly to retailers. After a worldwide search, Studios was chosen as the interior architect of key public spaces within the Mart.

The architects focused their design efforts on the central atrium, a 100 meter long, 50 meter high architectural canyon. Harnessing a seismic spine, they transformed it into a mega structure.

A red structural gridded wall extends the length of the atrium, protruding through a saw toothed roof of diagonal skylights, and penetrating the full height of the building's entry facade; serpentine perforated metal guard rails weave in and out of the wall's square opening. The wall grid punctures the space with brilliant color while it establishes a dramatic backdrop for a variety of bridges, elevators, escalators, and balconies. Into the theater-like spaces of the open grid, the architects integrated a cantilevered spiral stair clad in stainless steel, a one-person putting green on a balcony, and a two-story angled "bay window." In direct contrast to the movement of this wall, the architects established a long continuous curve of open floor plates on the opposing side of the atrium.

Making the most of a modest construction budget, Studios' design celebrates the circulation of the Center as a sculptural element. Spanning the atrium are three box-truss sky bridges. Glass enclosed elevator tubes soar full height at the far end, and miniature waterfalls drop almost nine meters from the Harbor Atrium to the entrance lobby.

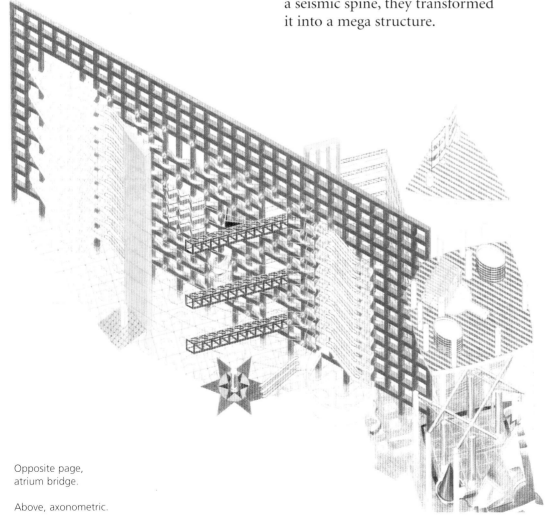

Opposite page,
atrium bridge.

Above, axonometric.

Below from left
to right, plan of the
roof, plan of a typical
upper level, and plan
of the second level.

Opposite page,
view of the
Main Atrium.

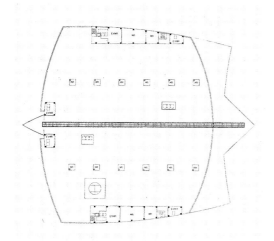 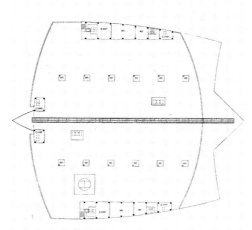 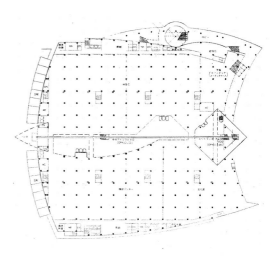

Right, longitudinal
section.

Below, view toward
the International Trade
Mart with the Retail
Complex on the right.

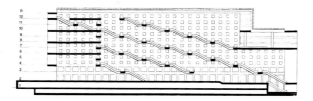

Below, Harbor Atrium.

Right, interior of the
Sky Bridge.

Below, view from
escalator.

Opposite page,
second escalator tower.

# McCann Erickson
# Advertising Agency
## San Francisco, California 1995

Aware of Studios' reputation for creating exciting workplaces for high-tech companies, the advertising agency McCann Erickson commissioned the architects to create an office that would project the agency's dynamic, progressive image. The 42,000-square-foot offices are located on three floors of an office tower in San Francisco's Financial District.

The design focused on the lobby and reception areas, challenging preconceived expectations of corporate high-rise interiors. The concrete floor and exposed overhead structure, in which customized aluminum indirect lighting fixtures cross the ceiling on a skewed axis, suggest the agency's unconventionality. Surrounding curvilinear plaster partitions layered with sheet metal panels, combine to create a compelling first impression for clients and visitors.

Studios reconfigured the back office space to promote open, interactive teamwork among staff members. The design of the new workplace was grounded in a desire for an environment conducive to the exploration of ideas, unhindered by hierarchy. At the core of the project is a central lounge area that simulates a family room where staff members can conduct informal working meetings, dine, relax, socialize, and exchange ideas. The result is a workplace that expresses the agency's new vision while projecting its revitalized spirit.

Opposite page,
view at main reception.

Right, plan of the
reception floor.

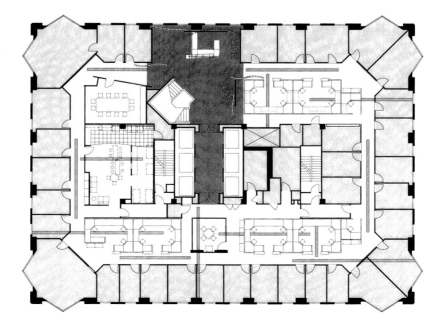

View from elevator
lobby.

Below, view at
conference room.

Bottom, employee
break area.

# Northern Telecom
## Santa Clara, California 1995

Northern Telecom, the Canadian-based telecommunications company, commissioned Studios to create a facility that could combine their long separated engineering and manufacturing facilities. Studio's program called for the addition of a 40,000 square-foot mezzanine within the existing 300,000 square-foot Silicon Valley manufacturing facility.

The architects unified the immense interior with a central atrium that functions as a "town square," where employees meet and the community's collaborative work takes place. The large room features mobile furniture, allowing several simultaneous meetings. As the venue for all-hands meetings and events, the atrium promotes the thriving culture of newly-merged departments.

The architects also created an S-shaped corridor that cuts diagonally through both levels, tying the facility's outlying reaches to the new atrium.

Curved yellow partitions were incorporated into the design vocabulary here, both to define the pathway and to enable employees to orient themselves within the labyrinthine space. A continuous neon tube running along the top of each wall whimsically accentuates the undulations of the path.

The design extends beyond the existing building envelope to signal that something new has taken place–a new entrance constructed out of a metal-framed prow was designed to emerge from the existing bland exterior. A boat-shaped glass and stucco structure encloses a monumental staircase, while a wing-like canopy shields the entry doors. The tapered passage leads employees from the lobby deep into the center of the middle building, intersecting the diagonal curve at the main internal street. The path ends at the two-story skylit atrium.

Opposite page, view of entry.

Left, plan of the ground floor and plan of the second floor.

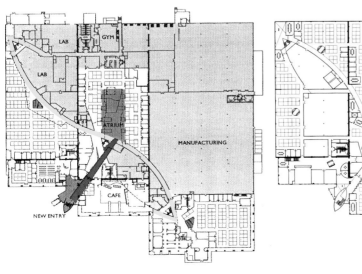

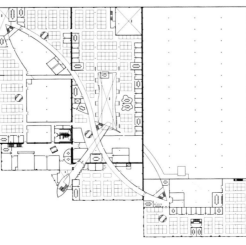

Entrance lobby.

Left, view of the Multi-purpose Atrium.

Below, stair at Multi-purpose Atrium.

# AirTouch Communications
## San Francisco, California 1995

AirTouch, a spin-off division of Pacific Telesis, is a major wireless communications company providing cellular phone services worldwide. One of the few large high-tech companies to remain in an urban center, AirTouch's 175,000-square-foot headquarters facility occupies eleven floors of a 31-story tower in the heart of San Francisco's Financial District. In designing this facility, Studios was challenged to create a workplace environment that would promote the company's forward-thinking creativity while at the same time respecting its blue-chip corporate roots.

The design goal was to achieve openness and connectivity on which technology companies thrive within the confines of a high-rise building. Studios knew from extensive experience in Silicon Valley that not

all creative work can be accomplished via e-mail or scheduled conferences; the social spaces they had established in other workplaces encouraged "out of the box" thinking, which reflected the goals of many of their progressive high-tech clients. For AirTouch, the architects strategically located the main reception area at the elevator-transfer level, to increase chance meetings by staff members situated on different floors and to render the high-rise spaces more social. The architects also located other employee-attracting facilities, such as video-conference rooms and central mail and copy centers, on this floor, creating a center for movement and interaction. With a central core established for social activity, the HVAC system and power, data and voice cabling were positioned

in columns set at the periphery of the building. Throughout the space, the architects maximized the use of natural light and left sight lines open to provide all employees with visual access to the spectacular views. Flexible areas, such as meeting spaces and open coffee bars were also incorporated into the plan to foster communication and positive social contact among employees.

An open, monumental stair between the executive level and the main customer and conferencing areas provides the opportunity for a product-exhibit wall. To avoid an "ivory tower" feeling in upgraded spaces, comparable finish materials and detailing were integrated throughout all levels of the project, as was the blue and gold of the AirTouch logo.

Opposite page, Demonstration room.

Below, from left to right, plan of 11th floor with Main Reception, plan of a typical office floor, and plan of 31st floor with Executive Support.

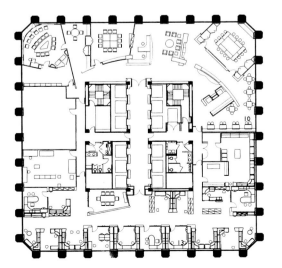 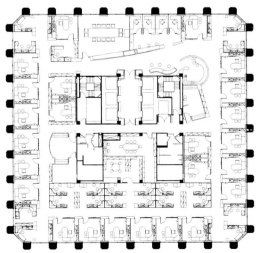 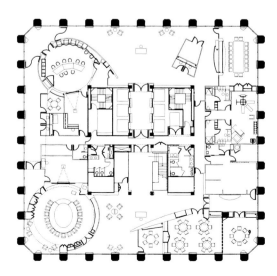

Left, from bottom up, exhibit area at Executive Support, Main reception area, and break out area.

Below, the boardroom.

# Société Générale
## Paris, France  1996

The twin towers of Société Générale's million-square-foot investment banking headquarters are located in La Défense, Paris. Société Générale commissioned Studios to design the interiors of the 40,000-square-foot corporate conference floor where all company-wide events take place.  The project features a 297 raked-seat assembly hall, a 260-seat brasserie/restaurant, and a variety of meeting rooms that accommodate twenty to sixty persons. In addition to the formal meeting spaces, Société Générale required a workplace that would encourage spontaneous discussions. Studios responded by establishing a clean, functional space that provided the sort of social space normally associated with public urban spaces.

Alluding to Baron Hausmann's redesign of Paris in the nineteenth century, the architects used the metaphor of a city to organize the vast floor plate.  Just as the Arc de Triomphe relates to the radiating avenues of the Etoile, circular stone-clad rotundas in each hemisphere of the floor are the focal points of the long, tapering corridors. The rotundas mediate the change of scale between the building's eight-story atrium and the smaller spaces of the conference center.

The wedge-shaped plan of the assembly hall follows the conspicuous triangular projection of the building's perimeter. The auditorium and its foyer and support facilities can function independently for company-sponsored civic activities.

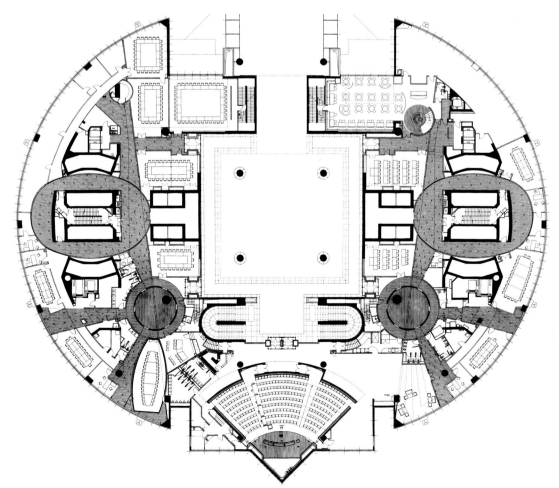

Opposite page, primary "Avenue" leading from Rotunda.

Left, plan.

Next spread, Brasserie stair, views of Rotunda, and auditorium.

View of secondary
passages.

Above, Brasserie.

Right, large conference
room.

# Arnold & Porter Headquarters
## Washington D.C. 1996

Arnold & Porter, one of the largest law firms in Washington D.C., has a liberal tradition dating back to its founding fifty years ago. In the design for its new headquarters, Arnold & Porter wanted to use the opportunity to rethink how law was practiced. Working with Arnold & Porter representatives, the architects embarked on a year-long study of "The Law Firm of the Future." This endeavor became the basis for selecting a site, configuring the base building, and developing its interior components.

Into what was once a speculative office building, Studios inserted an atrium to reflect the scale of the 400,000-square-foot project, and to act as a transition between the building's ersatz Beaux Arts facade and the contemporary aesthetic of the tenant improvements. A point of orientation for the interior's major programmatic elements, the atrium functions as an armature around which a kit of flexible components can be rearranged as the company grows and evolves.

Each of the 50,000-square-foot attorney floors is bisected by a main corridor, with exterior conference rooms on either end and "neighborhoods" of practice groups to either side. These neighborhoods were inspired by the group of town houses that originally housed the firm. Additionally, the architects displayed Arnold & Porter's extensive art collection in galleries connecting the atrium to the office spaces. To accommodate the Arnold & Porter tradition of end-of-day socializing, the architects created the Garden Room, an attorney lounge with a bar, fireplace, and television rooms. Prominently located on the top floor, the Garden Room's design also incorporates an interior staircase, which leads to an expansive roof terrace from where views of the Washington skyline can be enjoyed.

Opposite page, upward view of the Atrium.

Below, plans.

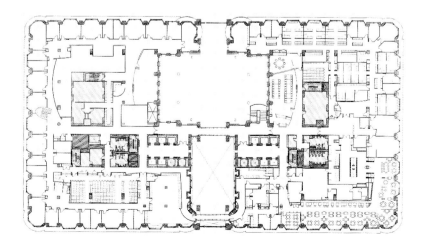

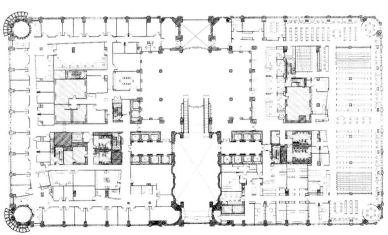

Below, Garden Room.

Right, Paul Porter
Conference Room.

# Discovery Communications, Inc.
## Miami, Florida 1997

Discovery Communications, a premier cable provider, commissioned Studios Architecture to develop a state of the art digital television production facility, capable of broadcasting simultaneously seven channels in three languages around the clock. In a user and visitor friendly environment, the design had to incorporate acoustically sensitive audio and visual production areas with master control and satellite transmission components, as well as office space for more than 200 creative and marketing staff. The project offered Studios an opportunity to implement some fundamental design strategies from their extensive work with high technology companies, along with their explorations of the future of the workplace.

The objective was to create a highly flexible environment conducive to collaborative work efforts. To meet this goal, the architects incorporated utility distribution elements constructed of recycled timber. Throughout the project, the design takes the edge off high-tech by embracing the use of technology in a humanistic context, rather than celebrating technology as an all-important object. The resulting energetic architectural expression celebrates the free thinking culture of Discovery Communications.

Opposite page, Audio layback suites.

Right, Master Control Room.

From bottom up,
plan of the first floor
(Broadcast), plan
of the second floor
(Post-production),
and plan of the third
floor (Creative).

Opposite page,
top, Transmission
Center; bottom,
Creative Group
Workspace.

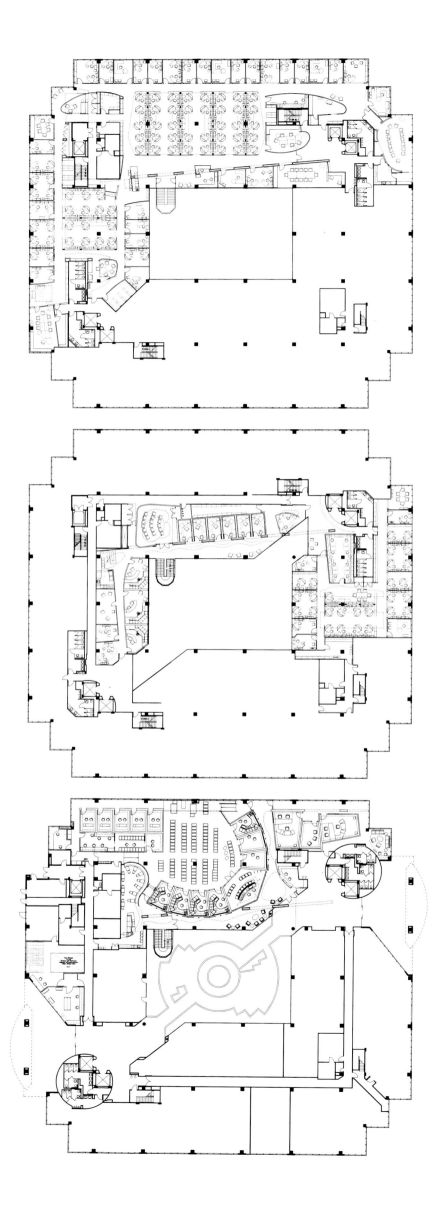

# Silicon Graphics, Inc.
# North Charleston Campus
## Mountain View, California 1997

This 500,000-square-foot campus was designed by Studios Architecture as an adjunct to Silicon Graphics' existing headquarters, occupied by the company since 1986. It was designed to provide a significant and unique architectural presence that would move beyond the architecturally indeterminate original facilities, anonymous concrete tilt-ups that were in no way evocative of Silicon Graphics' progressive culture and business philosophy.

Conceptually, the project functions like a high-tech interpretation of a medieval Tuscan hill town. Adopting the model of a small village, the architects arranged four articulated buildings around a landscaped courtyard. It was also designed to be a true campus, following the academic prototype, where pedestrian circulation is unhindered by vehicular traffic and groups of buildings have diverse architectural and programmatic relationships to one another. The complexity of the architectural density of the built project embodies the sort of socially active workplace environment more commonly found in urban settings; this was achieved in part by placing parking for 1,100 automobiles beneath a landscaped podium. By strategically punching holes through the ceiling plane, the architects were able to provide the underground parking facility with natural light and fresh air.

The buildings are clad in metal panels and glazed curtainwall, threaded with brick walls recalling the materials of the original Silicon Graphics facilities. Here the architects created a central plaza by arranging the two and three story buildings in a "U" shape. The various buildings were then connected at the second floor by bridges that underscore the architectural vocabulary and emphasize the sense of communitiy the architects hoped to establish. At the heart of the campus, in the main courtyard, lies the splintered-timber construct that houses the cafeteria, a space that doubles as a central all-hands meeting room. Adjacent to the dining facility is a curved element with clapboard siding, the "schoolhouse," which contains conference and training functions.

Silicon Graphics developed a five-acre public park adjacent to the project, and the architects encouraged public access through the site as part of a regional pedestrian-trail network. The main project entrance overlooks the new park, which has become emblematic of this project's integration of public and private space.

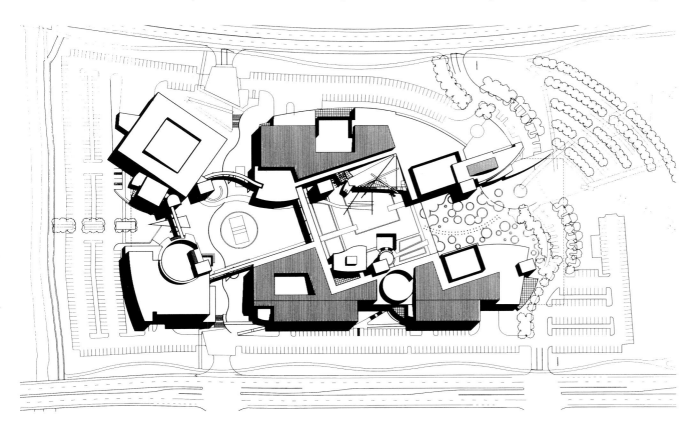

Opposite page, entry and Presentation Center.

Left, site plan.

Right, aerial view.

Below, plan of the
ground floor.

Bottom, plan of the
second floor.

Opposite page,
top, view
of "Schoolhouse".

Bottom, courtyard.

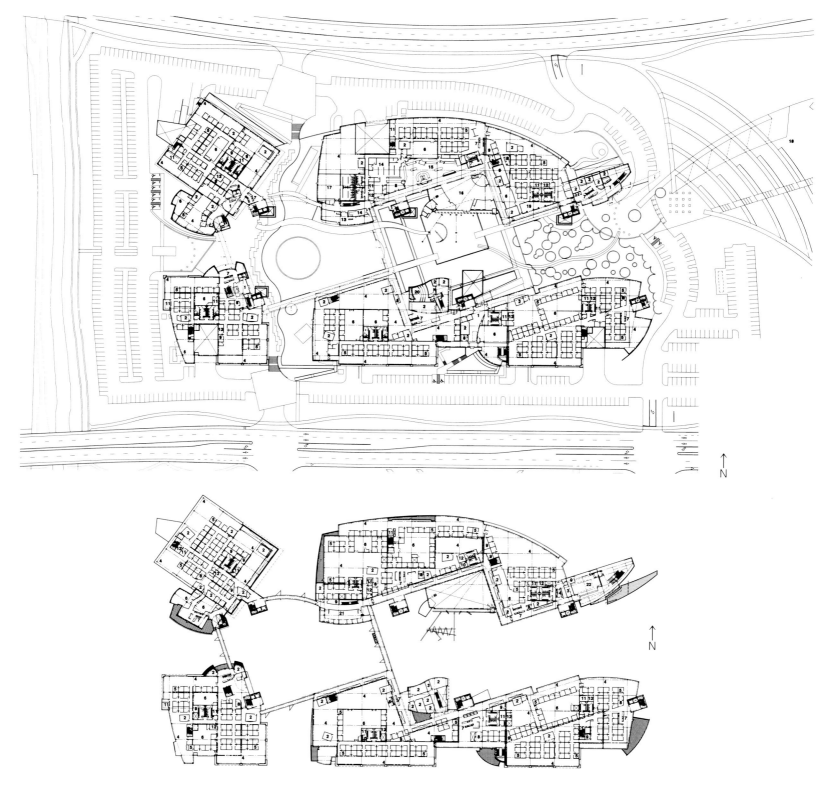

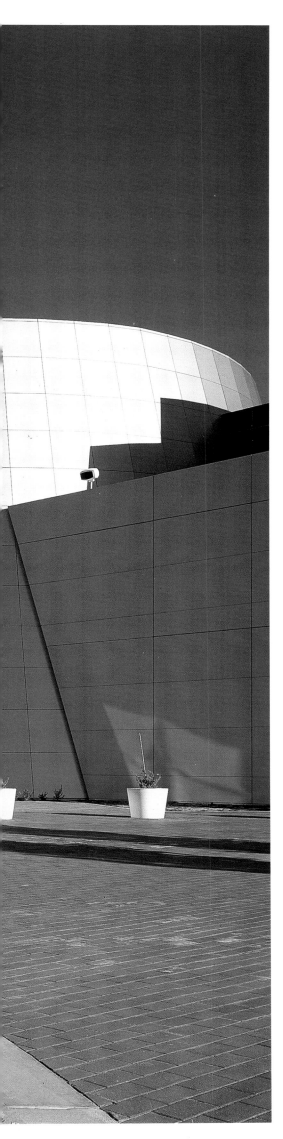

Left, western
pedestrian entry.

Below, Building 42.

Bottom, cafeteria.

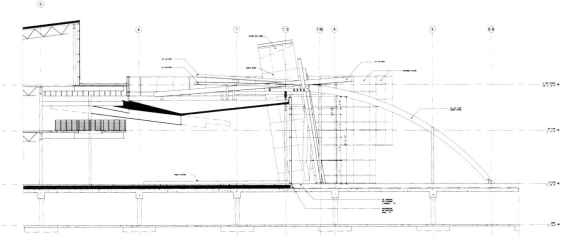

# Silicon Graphics, Inc. Crittenden Site
## Mountain View, California (unbuilt)

While it is famous for much of the technological innovation associated with the later part of the 20th Century, Silicon Valley is not known for significant architecture. Where companies come and go overnight and the exigencies of flexibility rule the landscape, it has been difficult for architects and their promise of permanence to make a great impact in this setting. For Silicon Graphics' Crittenden Campus, Studios intended not only to meet their client's growing space requirements and introduce innovative designs reflecting Silicon Graphics' culture and position in the Valley, but also to continue to raise the level of architectural discourse in an area where they had already done much work.

The 556,000-square-foot campus is located on a 25-acre parcel adjacent to Silicon Graphics' corporate headquarters. The site plan hinges on a central courtyard around which five two-story buildings are clustered, creating a focal community space within the campus for interaction and relaxation. Courtyard entrances and other common spaces are housed in small-scaled articulated elements behind which deep, amorphous floor plates for engineering and manufacturing are attached to a vast, tube-like pedestrian spine. The spine acts as the primary orientation device, visible from most points within the project and encourages employees to move between buildings. A tensile roofed cafeteria and a sculptural, multi purpose, 350-seat auditorium animate the courtyard, a focal point for the manufacturing and engineering communities.

Keeping in mind their client's need for flexibility, the architects designed the two larger buildings' ground levels for light manufacturing which can also be converted to host research and development, like the remainder of the campus, in the future. As they did in the nearby North Charleston campus, the architects also designed a single story parking podium that conceals most of the cars and protects the landscaped courtyard from vehicular circulation.

Opposite page, cafeteria.

Below, plan view of site model.

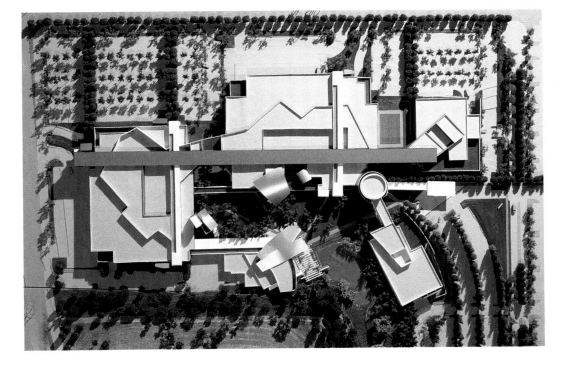

Model view at entry.

Below, view of entry
and auditorium.

Opposite page,
model view.

# FORE Systems Worldwide Headquarters
## Warrendale, Pennsylvania 1997

In 1995, when FORE Systems commissioned Studios Architecture to design its new manufacturing and research and development campus, it was one of the fastest-growing corporations in the United States. Like many of the Studios' Silicon Valley clients, FORE Systems was working on the leading edge of technological innovation. However, this innovator of ATM networking technology was laboring in relative obscurity in three non-descript buildings miles apart from each other, in the northern hills of Pittsburgh. In addition to increasing efficiency and promoting corporate identity, FORE Systems hoped that the new Studios-designed facility would function as an employee recruiting center to sustain their continuing expansion. The challenge for Studios was to capture the innovative yet informal culture that nurtured the young company during its meteoric growth, in a facility that would simultaneously refer to Pittsburgh's industrial heritage and compete with the high-tech facilities of the West Coast.

The architects' master plan called for five two-story structures, arranged side-by-side along a wooded, 96-acre ridge. The initial construction phase consisted of three buildings, comprising 300,000 square feet and housing 1,100 employees, penetrated and connected by an all-weather pedestrian link that extends for nearly a quarter of a mile. Building #3, in which the dining facility, fitness center, and manufacturing area are housed, was designed as the heart of the complex. Throughout the campus, the architects created areas that would encourage an inventive and productive workplace atmosphere while making employees comfortable.

The current three buildings are striking in that their walls do not follow standard architectural vocabularies, but instead create new relationships to the landscape as they lean in and out or organically curve. The main entrance, for example, in the first building closest to the long entrance drive, is composed of tilted clear glass. "It's a signature," said William J. Bates, FORE's director of facilities. "It's a statement that we're different and progressive, a clear signal to customers indicating new thinking on the cutting edge."

Emerging technology formed the conceptual basis for the proposed massive fifth building, which was designed to appear as though it were springing from the highest point on the ridge. The often erratic process of technological development informed the architecture of the other four structures; their designs are meant to suggest an evolution toward increasing weightlessness and transparency through alternating stages of chaos and order, kineticism and inertia.

Opening page
stair and elevator tipple
framed by social center.

Site plan with Building
1 on the left.

Main visitor entry plaza
at Buildings 1 and 2.

South elevation,
Building 2.

Left, entry of
Building 1.

Below, west wall
of Building 1.

Opposite page,
east employee entry
stair of Building 1.

Below, east elevation,
Building 1.

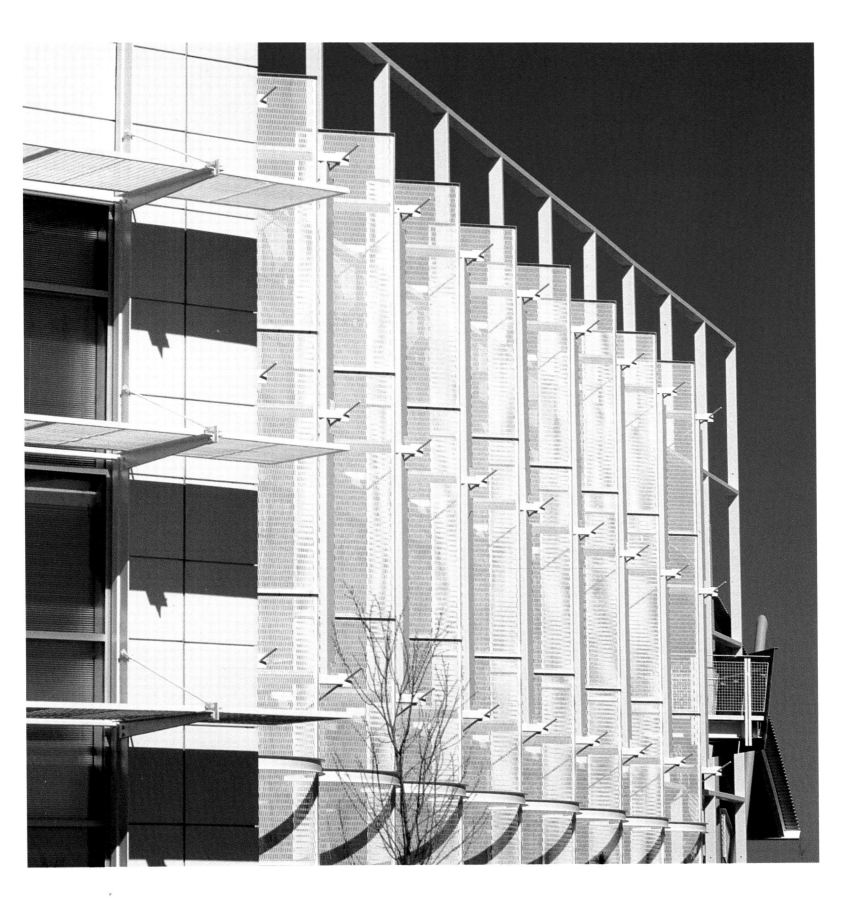

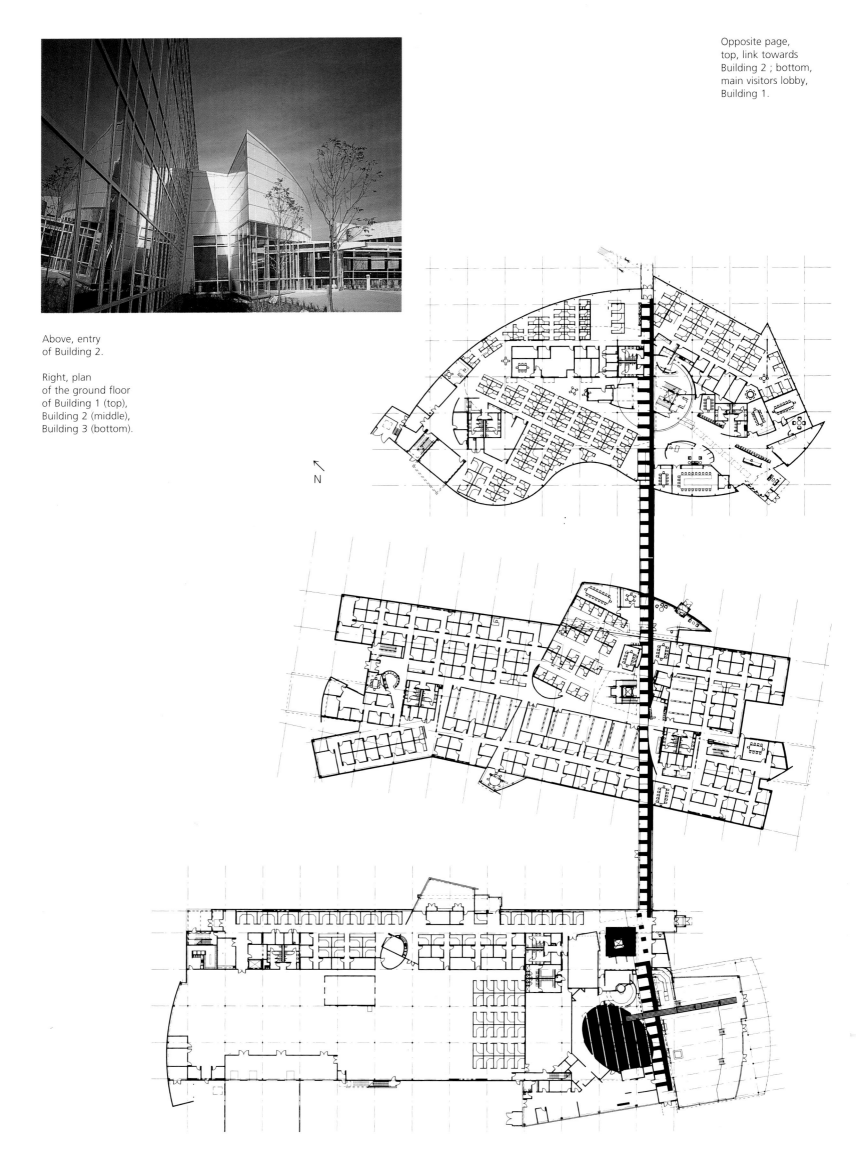

Opposite page,
top, link towards
Building 2 ; bottom,
main visitors lobby,
Building 1.

Above, entry
of Building 2.

Right, plan
of the ground floor
of Building 1 (top),
Building 2 (middle),
Building 3 (bottom).

N

# Shanghai Grand Theater
## People's Republic of China  1998

The Shanghai Grand Theater, located across from the People's Square in central Shanghai, is the result of an international design competition. Studios Architecture, in conjunction with Team 7 International, designed the interior architecture of this 1,800 seat hall to showcase opera, ballet, and symphonic performances.

Studios' program called for a three-tiered auditorium space incorporating the latest technology in stage design, theatrical lighting, and natural and electronic acoustics. The architects designed the curvaceous interior of the hall to deliberately contrast with the formal geometry of the building's exterior architecture; they created a warm, wooden element that seems to be cradled within the translucent glass and steel container. Without distinctions between form and function, much of the architectural vocabulary established here stems directly out of the need for a state-of-the-art facility.

The interior space, for example, was designed both for its acoustical characteristics and for its intimate seating configuration. The ceiling, a composition of individual curved plaster acoustical reflectors, was also designed as a visual screen for overhead catwalks for lighting access. Material selection also became a celebration of the space's function: the wooden ribbon-like balcony front and louvered baffles along the side walls add warmth to the space, while also enhancing the acoustics.

Following the tradition of grand theaters, the architects created a main lobby of dramatic architectural impact. The five-story space hosts a full height wall of golden, honed limestone, visible from the exterior through the transparent curtainwall, it acts as a backdrop for the theater's patrons as they ascend the double grand stair. With the lobby's visibility, the architects have added to the street theater of the People's Square, making a spectacle of activity both within the theater and in the open space outside. In addition to the performance hall and lobby, the 600,000 square foot building hosts an orchestra shell, rehearsal areas, dressing rooms, and other backstage facilities.

Opposite page, the Auditorium.

Right, VIP lobby.

133

Below, north-south
cross section.

Bottom, plan of the
main level.

Opposite page,
view of the main lobby.

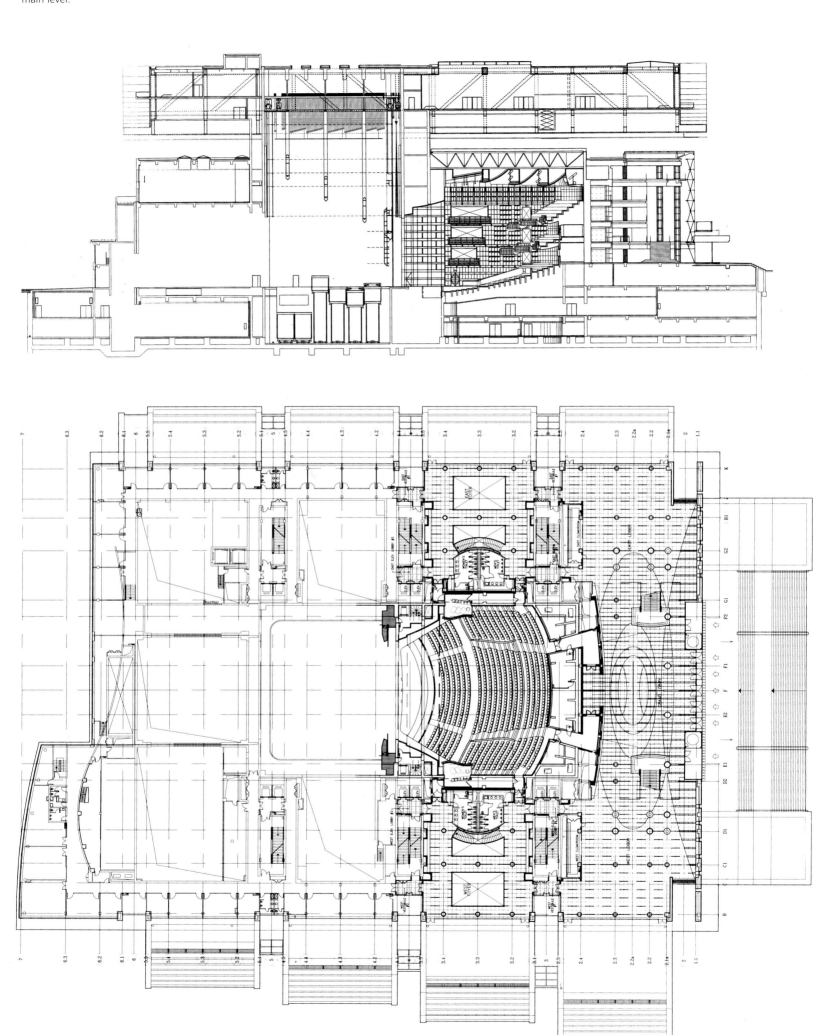

East-west section
at lobby.

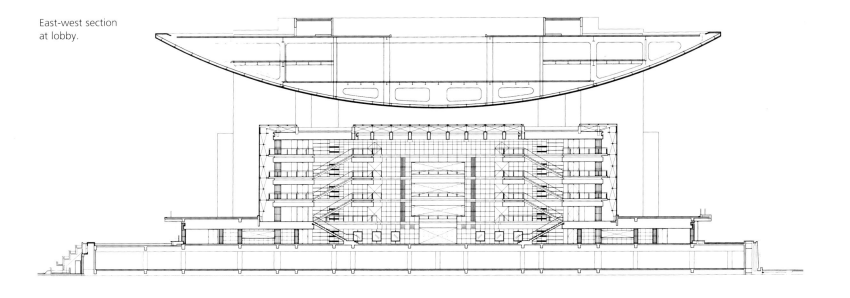

Auditorium.

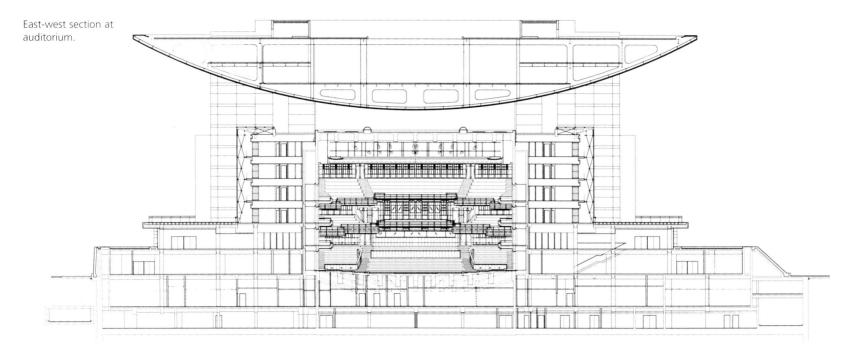

East-west section at
auditorium.

Auditorium design
model.

# 3Com Corporation Site X
## San Jose, California (unbuilt)

As they outgrow their existing corporate headquarters in Santa Clara, 3Com Corporation is working with Studios Architecture to plan a 72 acre, freeway frontage site for their new campus nearby. The 2.2 million square foot Studios' master plan consists of sixteen buildings for research and development and support, plus two parking structures. It is intended to serve as the architectural gateway to the rapidly developing San Jose North First Street High Tech Corridor.

For the Site X plan, the architects have established an assortment of smaller architectural components that, taken together, support the concept of the campus as a high-tech village. The goal is to recapture 3Com's original start-up mentality by providing an internally focused, nurturing environment and idea incubator.

The site plan is organized around a north-south open space that separates the initial two phases of the project and also provides emergency vehicle access deep within the complex. Common use facilities dining, fitness, and group meeting spaces are located here. The 570,000 square foot first phase presents a continuously curving wall to the freeway and on ramp. Rising above this plinth are broad, metal shed roofs, creating a dramatic mega-scaled profile to the passing traffic. These buildings will surround a courtyard developed above a parking podium.

To the west, the second phase was designed in a more linear configuration, with three buildings connected along a serpentine spine which telegraphs through their gabled roofs. Enclosing the opposite side of the meandering courtyard is a sinuously shaped parking structure.

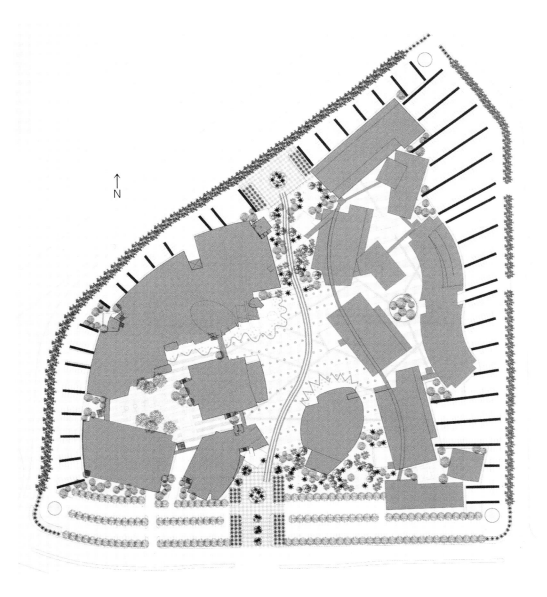

Opposite page, the main plaza.

Left, site plan.

Next spread, eastern view, southern entry view, freeway elevation, and western views of model.

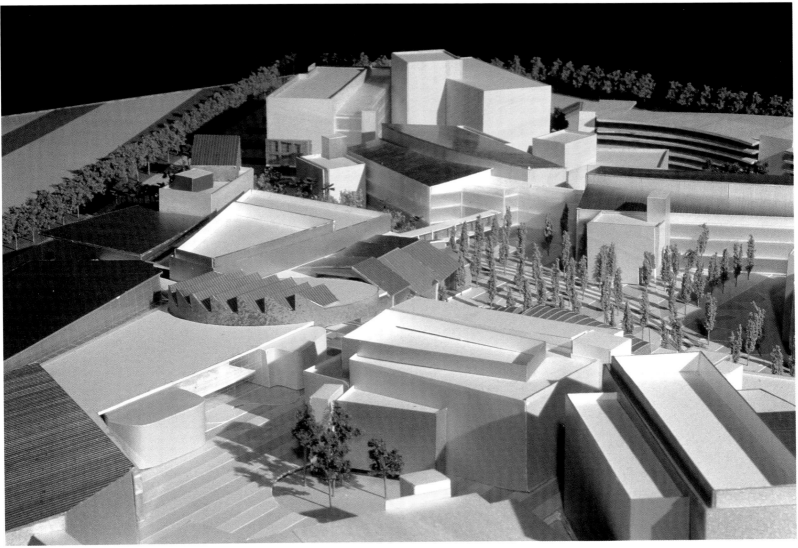

# List of Employees Present and Past Studios Architecture

Aarons, Steffani
Abraham, John P.
Adams, Jay C.
Adamson, Amy
Alderson, Nicholas
Alexander, Tarquin
Allen, Bruce
Amador, Guillermo E.
Ambrose, Jon
Amman, Smari
Anderson, Eric
Anderson, Gunnar H.
Andrews, Edward
Antoniades, Stala
Arana, Yordy
Aranaz, Todd
Aranda, Benjamin
Arenales, Oscar
Armsby, Robert H.
Arrasmith, Lori B.
Asaro, Larry
Askew, Yakuh
Aubry, Catherine
Baheti, Jyutika
Bailey, Patricia
Bailey, Ronald
Baker, Stephen
Bala, Julie
Bapst, Marielle
Barnhart, Terri
Baroni, Daniel
Barrett, Alex
Barrett, Cathy
Barrett, Debbie
Barrett, Jim
Bastianello, Domnik
Baz, Gisela
Beath, Fiona
Beatty, David
Béchet, Séverine
Becraft, Eric
Belcher, Nathaniel Q.
Bell, Michael
Bell, Patrick
Bennie, Christina
Benningfield, Jeffrey
Bens, Matthew
Beresford, James
Billet, Marc
Bini, Nicolo
Bisson Jr., Neil J.
Blomfield, Raewyn
Bloom, Jennifer
Bloomfield Jr., Frank
Blosen, Angela
Bolsega, Gerard
Borchardt, Kris
Boughan, Kieran
Boureau, Pascale
Bourke, D.
Bouvrie, Jacobus C.
Boyington, Alan D.
Bradsby, Bruce
Bradsby, Robert

Brehm, Matthew T.
Brewer, Leonard
Brown, Ivy
Brown, N. Darlene
Brown, Sonia
Bucholz, Merritt
Budd, Christopher J.
Buffington, Peter
Bullerdiek, Lynn F.
Burnett, Kirsty
Buten, Claire
Calvo, Jorge
Camp, Cynthia
Campbell, Julia
Campbell, Philip
Campuzano, Lauranne
Cannon, Sandra
Cardozo, Horacio
Castor, Daniel
Catey, Rebecca
Chambers, Stephen
Chang, Yung
Charalambous, Andrea
Chaska, Edie L.
Cheetham, Dan
Chemaly, Soraya L.
Chenault, Nancy
Cheung, Sabrina
Chiche, Dalia
Chin, William
Chottin, Jean-Pascal
Chow, Regina
Chu, Pietro
Claire, Kathleen
Clark, Consuella Re
Clark, Jonathan
Clayton, Shillest
Clement, Maureen
Collin, Arthur
Colson, Scott
Conners, Mark
Connors, Anne
Constantine, Stephanie
Cooperman, William
Cowey, James
Coyne, Courtney D.
Croom, Dolores L.
Cross, Susan
Crouzet, Jean Pascal
Crum, Timothy
Cullison, Cassandra
Cunningham, David
Curcio, Marie
Curry, Jeffrey W.
d'Arleux, Charlotte Morel
Dacus, Debra A.
Dakes, Steven C.
Danko, John R.
Danto-Sharpe, Valorie L.
Danzer Jr., Bruce Skiles
Davis, Steven
Dayvault, Mark
de Heeckeren, Alexandra
DeChambeau, Jason

DeChambeau, Sonja
Deegan, William
Deflumeri, Anthony
DeGarmo, Todd C.
Degnan, Kate
Denis, Arnaud
Dennehey, Jane
Devereaux, Cynthia
Dewitt, E. George
Diaz, Douglas
Dick, Jon
Dilworth, Charles
Do, Elizabeth
Doane, Babac
Dor, Tania
Dorsey, Debra G.
Doss, Annika
Douch, Sally
Downs, Jeanne
Drazin, Karen
Dubney, Mark
Ducrocq, Jean-Vincent
Dunn, Stephen
Dupont, Catherine
Dutro, Cynthia
Dworsky, Doug
Dwyre, Theresa
Eason, Katherine M.
Edmonds, Robert
Efstratiou, Clief
Estrada, Kevin
Evangelista, Florbela
Fahey, Liam
Fairbanks, Don W.
Fea, Prue
Fears, William
Ferry, Kristen
Fichtner, Birgit
Fischer, William A.
Fong, Jaden
Ford, Matthew
Foster, Allen
Foster, Rebecca
Fox, Robert D.
Foyer, Michele
Frantz, Joan
Freed, Eliot
Frost, Dana
Fuentevilla, Miguel
Gabriel, Karyn
Gaffney, Dennis G.
Galli, Carla
Gardner, John
Garner, Noel
Garrigoux, Raphaële
Gentilucci, Pamela S.
Gentilucci, Scott
Geraghty, Robert
Gerrety, James
Gibbard, Roland
Gibson, Jennifer M.
Gifford, Sarah
Girling, C.
Glomset, Leif

Godfree, Andy
Golden, David
Gong, Michelle
Gonzalez, Sonia
Goodrich, Abram
Goodwin, Bruce
Goren, Leora
Gota, James
Graham, Jennifer G.
Grant, Clare
Grechi, Andres
Greer, Sara
Griffin, Jerry
Grisso, Ashley
Gross, Samuel H.
Gruenhut, Wendy
Guittard, Jay
Guzman, Ana C.
Haegglund, Kelly
Hahn, Joanna
Hamlet, Kathy L.
Haney, David
Hanson, Karen A.
Hapstak, Peter
Harcourt, Anna
Harper, Marian
Hawkins, Alistair
Hayes, Alexander
Hayes, Cynthia
Hayes, David
Heckert, Kristen
Heimerman, Kathleen
Helgeson, Carly B.
Helm, William
Hench, Anders A.
Henderson, John
Herrmann, Allan
Hershey, Mathew
Hevrdejs-Clarke, Merrie
Hewitt, Abiguel
Hewitt, Ann
Hicks, Kyle
Hollis, Matthew
Hong, Yung Un
Horchman, Marc H.
Horne, Alison
Howe, Sabret A.
Hruby, Daniel
Ingram, Jill
Irving, Richard
Irwin, Lisa A.
Irwin, Sean
Irwin, Sherri L.
Jacob, Esther
Jacobs, Linda
Jacobs, Sonia
Jacobsen, Diana
Jacobsen, Ingrid
Jacobsen, Kari
Jansen, Joseph
Janus, Wendy
Jefferies, Martin
Jennings, Paul
Jensen, Kevin W.

Jensen, Steven David
Johnson, Erick
Jones, Bonnie
Jones, G Wesley
Jones, Victor
Kaczmarowski, James
Kanda, Noriyuki
Kasten, John F.
Katzman, Lyn
Kearney, Timothy
Keilp, Jennifer M.
Kelly, Brian
Kerns, Jolie
Khouri, Bradley
Kim, Helen E.
Kindlon, Gordon
King, Jeffrey
Kinley, Paul
Kinley, Paula
Klancher, Robert J.
Klober, Wolf-Dietrich
Klomp, Brian Q.
Knapton, Cynthia
Knowles, John
Knudson, David
Ko, Shiou-Hee
Koehne, Katherine M.
Koehne, Laura A.
Koenig-Johnson, Karen
Kohn, Laurie
Kolb, Mary
Krieger, Rhonda
Krizmanic, Thomas R.
Kronlokken, Connie
Kuebler, Carolinn
Kupka, Cynthia
Kustin, Ira P.
Landry, Joseph A.
Lane, Patricia
Langberg, Lars
Larkin, Timothy J.
Lausten, Susan E.
Lavia, Juliet
Lawton, Melissa C.
Lee lll, Robert E.
Lee, Christina
Lee, Jason
Lee, Mildred
Lee, Ming
Lee, Robert J.
Lefeubvre, Tessa
Leibovitz, Geoffrey
Leitch, Christopher
Lentz, Scott
Leon, Patricia C.
Leon, Thomas G.
Leonard, R. Bruce
Leonhardt, Robert J.
Lepori, Pedro
Leroy, Sylvie
Leung, Monica
Lew, Stanley
Lieggi, Michelle
Lindahl, Lee A.

Lipson, Peter
Little, Louise
Locascio, Kenneth
Logue, Michael
Long, Steve
Lopez, Monica
Lourenço, Josiane
Lovett, Sally P.
Lovette, Martha
Luis, Daniel A.
Luo, Philip S.
Maassen, Werner
MacDonald, Heather
MacDonald, Iain
MacDonald, Stuart
MacEwen, Alan B.
Madgwick, Sara
Maese, Maricela
Malbaff, Sonja L.
Manning, Kim E.
Manning, Margaret J.
Mantz, Gregory
Manwinder, Lall
Marcus, Kenneth G.
Marinaro, Pat
Markel, Christopher
Marley, Elizabeth
Martens, Andra
Martin, Elizabeth
Martin, Isaiah
Martin, Lynn
Masson, Michael
Matko, Anna K.
McCarthy, Jason
McCarthy, Michelle
McClure, Rhonda
McDaniel, Brian
McGlone, Kathryn
McGlynn, Michael
McIntyre, Jonathan
McMurtrie, Darren
McNamara, Joseph J.
McNamara, Robin P.
Meaker-Joseph, Gail
Meis, Daniel R.
Mercury, Suzanne
Meyer, Frédérique
Meyer, James
Michaels, Tony
Milina, Mark
Milkowski, Tiffonie
Miller, Ann
Miller, Gina M.
Miller, Mason
Minch, Nathan
Mitchell, Christopher
Mitschkowetz, Elena
Mixon, Elaina
Mobraaten, Darcy
Moffat, Abby S.
Molina, Marc
Mommaels, Fabienne
Monson, Alexis
Moretz, David

Morrison, Paul
Mostert, Kamala L.
Mouradian, Anne
Mulcahy, John
Murray, Margaret
Murray, Teresa Lynne
Nakib, Noha
Napell, Gail
Nashed, Robert
Neel, Bertrand
Newby, Melissa
Ngiam, Ronald
Nielsen, Barry
Nienberg, Nancy
Nilo, Joyce
Nilsen, Gerald
Niner, Fred
Nitzan, Galia
Norton, Brett
Nowicki, Teresa
O'Brien, Leo J.
O'Callahan, Michael
O'Connell, Joseph R.
O'Reilly, Thomas
Odubanjo, Femi
Ogorzalek, David
Old, G. Christina
Oleson, Douglas
Olson, Phillip
Ortega, Joe
Ostoya, Jacek K.
Overman, Connie
Pacheco, Maria
Palermo,Mark
Panico, Andrea
Papanastasia, Koula
Parco, Ben
Parkinson, Laurie K.
Pasquier, Gilles
Pastellas, Pierre
Patterson, Jennifer
Paxton, Carter Cobb
Payne, Craig
Perez, Shirley
Perkins, Kara
Peterson, Cliff
Peterson, Heidi
Petzke, Kathleen M.
Pfeiffer, Deborah
Piankoff, Julienne C.
Pierandrei, Pier
Pinkowski, Tom
Pinto, Nadine
Piotrowska, Kasia
Piper, David
Pires, Remy
Pitiot, Stéphane
Pitt, Cynthia
Pope, Jeannie
Porter, Sean
Portz, Jesse
Powell, JoAnne
Prusinski, Thomas
Pulley, Richard

Pyne-Hanley, Shelley
Quattrone, James M.
Quezada, Alfred
Quirk, Brian
Race, Linda
Rae, Gene
Rafik, Salim
Ramos, Jason H.
Raskin,Jay
Rauser, Eric
Raverdel, Monique
Rboul, Jamal
Reardon-Smith, Yetta
Redding, Tiffany
Redon, Isabelle
Reese, Janeen
Reid, John
Reinhold, Schneider
Rhines, Lauren
Riano, Maria
Ribas-Artze, Olga
Rice, Stephanie
Richards, Douglas R.
Richvalsky, Joe
Robb, Janet
Roberson, Darryl T.
Roche, Mark
Rockstroh, Peggy
Rogge, Chris
Rosar, Kateri
Rose, Michael S.
Ross, Delisa V.
Ross, Michael
Rothman, Simone S.
Rousseau, Christine
Rubbo, Gregory
Ruddy, Janet
Rugg, Lawrence
Ruph, Catherine
Russell, Tori
Rybkowski, Zosia K.
Sabalvaro, David
Salamone, Sherri
Sales, Carey C.
Saliba, Lisa
Salibian, Gassia
Salles, Denise
Salter, Hayden
Samalot, Monica
Sargeson, Alex
Saunders, Bruce R.
Saunders, Mathew
Savage, Elizabeth
Schmidt, Jeffrey A.
Schneiderman, Marc D.
Schulz, Rhonda A.
Schwartz, Reuben
Scull, Peter B.
Selkregg, Candace
Sessoms, Beverly
Shearer, Alistair
Shearer, Jeanette
Shelhorse, Joseph E.
Shepherd, Bobby

Sherman, Fredric
Shewring, Leslie
Shirley, Martin
Shvetsky, Isabella
Sibert, Annika
Simmons, Linda
Simpkins, Peter
Sinclair, Linda
Skaggs, Bradley
Smith, Kristin T.
Smith, Mitch
Snellgrove, Simon
Solis, Kathryn
Spencer, Abby A.
Spielman, Peter
Spielmann, Pit
Spirtos, Linda H.
Sporer, Elisabeth
Springuel, Yves B.
Stallings, Amy
Stanley, Gwen
Starr, Iryse
Stelmarski, Ronald
Stewart, Dale A.
Stewart, Gerry
Storning, Allan
Strader, Lynda
Straja, André
Strasser, Claire M.
Stubb, Peter
Subramanian, Ravindran
Sueberkrop, Erik
Sugarman, Leon
Sullivan, Dennis
Tacart, Nathalie
Talim, Jimmy
Tate, Patricia
Taylor, Steven
Tekisalp, Erhan
Terzian, Leslie
Tether, Majorie
Thiery, Philippe
Thomas, Liane
Thomas, Richard S.
Thompson, Mark
Thompson, Raymond
Thorne, Christopher
Thornley, Connie
Tobin, Anna
Tolman, Brian
Tom, Alan
Tomioka, Chizuru
Tompkin, Gervais
Tong, Jennifer
Tran, Vy
Trimble, Diana
Troitzsch, Matthias
Trujillo, Walter
Tse, Caroline
Turmala, Carole
Turner, Vikkii
Udall, Chris
Vahle, Luke
Vail, Crystale

Vali, Erin
Van Gool, Robert
VanDINE, Peter D.
Venissat, Helene
Veron-Durand, Valérie
Verwers, Todd
Viall, Debra
Vidal, Maria G.
Villani, Olivier
Villegas, Alexandra
Vincent, Stephania
Vinson, George A.
Vlachos, Mona C.
Waddell, Andy
Wagner, David
Walker, Colin
Wallack, Linda S.
Wallis, Neil
Walton, Lilian
Warasila, John
Waschitz, Scott
Waters, Patrick
Wayne, Sean
Weaver, Angela
Webb, Apryl D.
Weber, Michael E.
Weber, Robert
Welschmeyer, Paul W.
Wenzel, Maria B.
Wesely, George
Wheeler, Jeff
Wichman, Ron
Willard, Lawson
Williams, Monique
Williams, Scott
Willmer, Sarah
Willow, Thomas
Winkhart, Jeff
Winslow, Elizabeth A.
Winterich, Daniel J.
Wong, Clifford A.
Woo, May
Wynne, John G.
Yardley, Martin
Yee, Thomas
Yori, Robert
Zandhuis, Angelique
Zeidner, Russell
Zimola, Judy
Zivy, Dominique
Zweifel, Mark F.

# Credits

*Projects illustrated in "Power of the Pragmatic" book:*

STUDIOS Architecture
San Francisco, California
*Structural Engineer:*
GFDS Engineers
*Lighting:* Architecture & Light
*Photographer:*
Michael O'Callahan

Nike Showroom and Sales Office
New York, New York
*MEP Engineer:* Flack & Kurtz
*Lighting Consultant:* Horton Lees
*Photographer:* Andrew Bordwin

Bankgesellschaft Berlin
Berlin, Germany
*Architect of original 1930 Building:*
Peter Behrens
*Base Building Architect:*
Pysall, Strahrenberg & Partners
*Acoustical Consultant:*
Büro Reichard
*MEP & IT:* IB Heimann, Integ,
and Flack & Kurtz
*Photographer:* Christian Kerber

Hanley-Wood, Inc.
Washington D.C.
*Structural Engineer:*
Fernandez & Associates
*MEP Engineer:* GHT Limited
*Lighting Designer:*
Johnson Schwinghammer
*Photographer:* Paul Warchol

*Works*

Apple Computer
Various Interiors
Cupertino, California

Apple Advanced Computer
Technology Center
*MEP Engineer:*
Glumac International
*Lighting:* Horton Lees,
STUDIOS Architecture,
and Glumac International
*Millwork:*
Limited Production Inc.
*Acoustical Consultant:* ACI
*Photographer:* Paul Warchol

Apple Learning Center
*Structural Engineer:*
GFDS Engineers
*Mechanical Engineer:*
Courries & Okamoto, Inc.
*Electrical:*
The Engineering Enterprise
*Audio Visual:*
Lude Broadcast Engineering,
EISI Communication Technology
*Photographers:*
Sharon Risedorph, Tom Bonner

Apple Research & Design
Buildings 2 & 5
*Base Building Architect:* HOK
*Acoustical Consultant:*
Charles M. Salter Associates, Inc.
*Lighting Designer:*
Auerbach & Associates
*Structural Engineer:*
GFDS Engineers
*Photographer:* Mark Darley/ Esto

Apple Fitness Center
*Structural Engineer:* Rudolf Fehr
*Mechanical Engineer:*
ICOM (Design Build)
*Photographers:*
Colin McRae, Chas McGrath

Silicon Graphics, Inc.
Various Interiors
Mountain View, California

Silicon Graphics Building 6
*Lighting Designer:*
Darrell Hawthorne
*Structural Engineer:*
GFDS Engineers
*AudioVisual:*
Paoletti and Associates
*Photographer:* Paul Warchol

Silicon Graphics Building 8
*Structural Engineer:*
GFDS Engineers
*Mechanical:*
Glumac International
*Photographer:* Paul Warchol

Silicon Graphics Building 9
*Structural Engineer:*
GFDS Engineers
*Mechanical:*
ACCO (Design/ Build)
*Photographer:* Paul Warchol

Silicon Studio
*Structural Engineer:*
Tom Johnson Associates
*Mechanical:* ACCO
*Photographer:*
Michael O'Callahan

3Com Corporation
Headquarters
Santa Clara, California
*Landscape Architect:*
Ken Kay, Phase I;
Peter Walker Partners,
Phases II & III
*Structural Engineer:*
Structural Design Engineers
*Lighting Designer:*
Architecture & Light
*MEP:* Ajmani & Pamidi, Inc.
(Criteria Engineer Phase I);
Alfa Tech (Phases II & III)
*Photographers:* Tim Hursley,
Richard Barnes, Michael
O'Callahan

University of California, Davis
Alumni & Visitors Center
Davis, California
*Landscape Architect:* Antonia Bava
*Structural Engineer:*
Structural Design Engineers
*Lighting Designer:*
Auerbach & Associates
*Mechanical Engineer:*
Ajmani Associates
*Electrical Engineer:*
Takahashi Engineers
*Photographer:* Paul Warchol

Knoll International GmbH
Showroom
Frankfurt, Germany
*Specialty Metalwork:*
Limited Productions, Inc.
*Lighting Designer:*
Lighting Design Partnership
*Electrical Engineer:* Wero
*Photographer:* Engelhardt & Sellin

3Com Corporation
Dublin, Ireland
*Production Architect:*
Brian O'Halloran & Associates
*Structural Engineer:*
Ove Arup & Partners

*MEP Engineer:* Delap & Waller
*Quantity Surveyor:*
Keogh McConnell
*Photographers:* Chris Gascoigne,
Michael O'Callahan

Apple Computer
United Kingdom
London, England
*Base Building Architect:*
Troughton McAslan
*MEP:* Ove Arup & Partners
*Quantity Surveyor:*
Davis Langdon & Everest
*Photographer:* Paul Warchol

Silicon Graphics, Inc.
Shoreline Entry Site Building
Mountain View, California
*Landscape Architect:*
The SWA Group
*Structural Engineer:*
GFDS Engineers
*MEP:* ENCON
*Civil Engineer:*
Sandis Humber Jones
*Acoustics:*
Charles M. Salter Associates, Inc.
*Lighting Designer:* Lumenworks
*Photographers:* Richard Barnes,
Michael O'Callahan, Paul
Warchol

International Trade Mart
Osaka, Japan
*Base Building Architect:*
Nikken Sekkei
*Lighting Consultant:*
S. Leonard Auerbach Associates (US)
Rise Lighting Design Office (Japan)
*Photographers:*
Akihiro Kawamura, SS Osaka;
Seishi Maeda, Shinwa Jitsugyo Inc.;
Erik Sueberkrop, FAIA

McCann Erickson Advertising
Agency
San Francisco, California
*Lighting Consultant:*
Architecture & Light
*Photographer:* Michael O'Callahan

Northern Telecom
Santa Clara, California
*Structural Engineer:*
Cecil H. Wells, Jr. and Associates
*MEP:* Alfa Tech Bouillon
and Air Systems
*Photographer:*
Michael O'Callahan

AirTouch Communications
San Francisco, California
*Lighting Designer:*
Architecture & Light
*MEP Engineer:*
Glumac International
*Acoustical Consultant:*
Charles M. Salter Associates, Inc.
*Structural Engineer:*
Glumac International
*Photographer:* Chas McGrath

Société Générale
Paris, France
*Base Building Architect:*
Cabinet Andrault-Parat
*Mechanical & Electrical:*
SARI Maintenance
*Photographers:* Luc Boegly,
Jean-Philippe Caulliez

Arnold & Porter
Washington D.C.
*Base Building Architect:*
Keyes Condon Florence
*Lighting Designer:*
Johnson Schwinghammer
*MEP Engineer:* Flack & Kurtz

*Acoustical Engineer:*
Shen, Milsom & Wilke
*Photographer:* Paul Warchol

Discovery Communications, Inc.
Miami, Florida
*Structural Engineer:*
Martinez Kreh Associates
*MEP Engineer:*
Cosentini Associates
*Acoustical Engineer:*
Russ Berger Design Group
*Photographer:* Paul Bardagjy

Silicon Graphics, Inc.
North Charleston Campus
Mountain View, California
*Landscape Architect:*
The SWA Group
*Structural Engineer:*
GFDS Engineers
*MEP Criteria Engineer:* ENCON
*Civil Engineer:*
Sandis Humber Jones
*Acoustics:*
Charles M. Salter Associates, Inc.
*Lighting Designer:* Lumenworks
*Photographers:* Richard Barnes,
Dennis Morris, Michael
O'Callahan, Steve Whittaker

Silicon Graphics, Inc.
Crittenden Site
Mountain View, California
*Photographer:*
Michael O'Callahan

FORE Systems Worldwide
Headquarters
Warrendale, Pennsylvania
*Associated Architect:*
Perfido Weiskopf Architects
*Landscape Architect:* GWSM, Inc.
*Structural Engineer:*
Gensert Bretnall Associates
*Lighting Designer:*
Architecture & Light
*Photographers:* Richard Barnes,
Lockwood Hoehl

Shanghai Grand Theater
People's Republic of China
*Associated Architect:*
Team 7 International
*Base Building Architect:*
Arte Charpentier & Associates
*Local Architect:*
East China Architectural Design
& Research Institute
*Lighting Consultants:*
Auerbach & Glasow
and Horton Lees
*Acoustical Consultant:*
Kirkegaard & Associates
*Theater Lighting:*
ADB International and Advanced
Communication Equipment Co.,
Ltd.
*Photographers:* Roger Lee,
Kerun Ip

3Com Corporation Site X
San Jose, California
*Structural Engineer:*
Structural Design Engineers
*Landscape Architect:*
Peter Walker Partners
*Photographer:*
Michael O'Callahan

Varet Marcus & Fink
Washington D.C.
*M/E/P Engineers:*
B & A Consulting Engineers
*Lighting Consultant:*
Coventry Lighting
*Photographer:*
Paul Warchol